SPOOKY
Canada

SPOOKY
Canada

*Tales of Hauntings, Strange Happenings,
and Other Local Lore*

RETOLD BY S. E. SCHLOSSER

ILLUSTRATED BY PAUL G. HOFFMAN

INSIDERS' GUIDE®

GUILFORD, CONNECTICUT
AN IMPRINT OF THE GLOBE PEQUOT PRESS

INSIDERS'GUIDE®

Text design by Lisa Reneson
Illustrations and map border by Paul G. Hoffman
Map by Lisa Reneson © Morris Book Publishing, LLC

ISBN 978-0-7627-4560-9

Library of Congress Cataloging-in-Publication Data is available.

Manufactured in the United States of America
First Edition/Second Printing

For Brenda, who shared my adventures and misadventures each summer when I visited Quebec.

For the Draper family—Ron, Mary, Lorraine, Deb, Bev, Brian, Brenda, Tim, and their families. Thank you for the warm welcome you extended each summer to the Schlossers.

For my family—David, Dena, Tim, Arlene, Hannah, Emma, Nathan, Ben, Deb, Gabe, Clare, Jack, Chris, Karen, and Davey.

And for Mary, Paul, Kaleena, and all the wonderful Globe Pequot staff who work on the Spooky series—with my thanks!

* * *

Contents

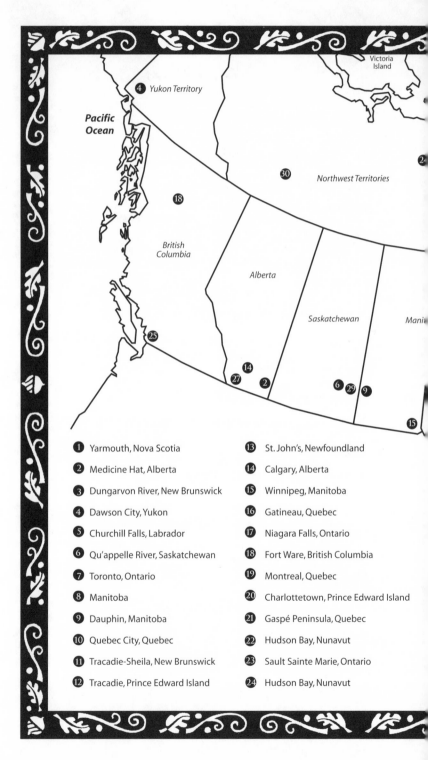

Victoria Island

④ Yukon Territory

Pacific Ocean

㉚ Northwest Territories

⑱

British Columbia

Alberta

Saskatchewan

Mani...

㉕

⑭
㉗ ②

⑥ ㉙ ⑨

⑮

❶ Yarmouth, Nova Scotia

❷ Medicine Hat, Alberta

❸ Dungarvon River, New Brunswick

❹ Dawson City, Yukon

❺ Churchill Falls, Labrador

❻ Qu'appelle River, Saskatchewan

❼ Toronto, Ontario

❽ Manitoba

❾ Dauphin, Manitoba

❿ Quebec City, Quebec

⓫ Tracadie-Sheila, New Brunswick

⓬ Tracadie, Prince Edward Island

⓭ St. John's, Newfoundland

⓮ Calgary, Alberta

⓯ Winnipeg, Manitoba

⓰ Gatineau, Quebec

⓱ Niagara Falls, Ontario

⓲ Fort Ware, British Columbia

⓳ Montreal, Quebec

⓴ Charlottetown, Prince Edward Island

㉑ Gaspé Peninsula, Quebec

㉒ Hudson Bay, Nunavut

㉓ Sault Sainte Marie, Ontario

㉔ Hudson Bay, Nunavut

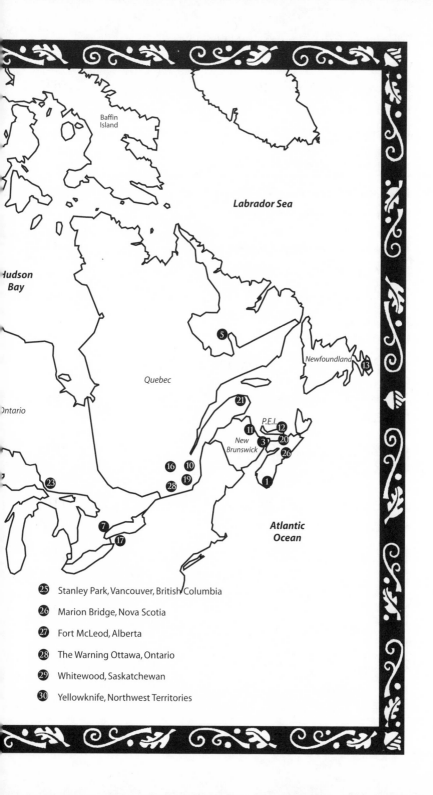

Baffin
Island

Labrador Sea

Hudson
Bay

⑤

Newfoundland

⑬

Quebec

Ontario

㉑

New
Brunswick

P.E.I.

⑪ ⑫

③ ⑳

⑯ ⑩ ㉖

㉘ ⑲

㉓

①

Atlantic
Ocean

⑦

⑰

㉕ Stanley Park, Vancouver, British Columbia

㉖ Marion Bridge, Nova Scotia

㉗ Fort McLeod, Alberta

㉘ The Warning Ottawa, Ontario

㉙ Whitewood, Saskatchewan

㉚ Yellowknife, Northwest Territories

CONTENTS

CONTENTS

Introduction

When I was two years old, my father learned of a fishing-and-hunting lodge up in the Gatineau River region of Quebec. Deciding this would make a great family vacation spot, he packed up my Mom, me, and my six-week-old brother and hauled us north to Victoria Lodge, where he rented a cabin on the lake. Literally, on the lake. You could fish from the front porch, and if you slipped climbing the rail, you would fall right into the water. I should know. I nearly gave my mother a heart attack with that trick!

My Mom learned a lot on that first trip to Canada. She learned that my father was so obsessed with fishing that he would stick a fishing pole into the playpen with his six-week-old baby and urge him to "reel it in, son" when a sunfish bit the line. She learned that her toddler (me) was irresistibly drawn to water and had to be watched every single minute. She learned what it was like to drive on dirt roads and that it would be useless to wash the car until we returned home. She also learned that the wonderful lady who was the lodge cook and the wife of the owner had a sympathetic ear and would be happy to chat with a "fishing widow," swapping recipes and watching to make sure the red-haired toddler-girl didn't drown herself in the little swimming area in front of the lodge. Somehow, my Mom survived that first trip to Quebec, and the Gatineau lakes region became a favorite family vacation spot thereafter.

As a little girl, Victoria Lodge became synonymous with

Canada for me. Long after we crossed the border each year, I would ask my poor parents when we would be in Canada. "We are in Canada," they told the stubborn little girl in the back seat. "No, we're not," I'd respond, shaking my head at such foolishness. "Canada" didn't start for me until we arrived in Gracefield and crossed the narrow bridge leading to the back roads that took us to Northfield, Quebec, and Victoria Lodge.

Image my surprise when I finally learned that Canada was much larger than one small town! When I came to grips at last with the concept of geography, I was amazed at the vastness of this fair land and the variety of its topography. From the Maritime Islands and thick forests in the east to the vast Rocky Mountains range in the west, and away up north to the tundra and the ice fields of the arctic, Canada looms large and mysterious and quite wonderful.

If I thought the country itself was magnificent, I found the people even more so. Some of the very best friends our family will ever have we met on our summer trips to Quebec. One fellow we know once delayed supper to drive his farm tractor several miles down the road in order to help the Schlossers pull their car out of the Mill Pond, where it sat up to the back bumper in water. (Don't ask! Just *don't ask!*) And year after year, our favorite guide patiently took my father and each of his growing children to the best fishing spots on the lake and cooked us the most amazing shore lunches in the entire world.

Over the decades, many of the people in our favorite vacation spot welcomed our rather crazy American family into their hearts, their homes, and their lives. They watched over my siblings and me as children, helped guide us through the confusing teen years, and rejoiced with us as our family expanded to include new spouses and grandchildren. I owe them more than I can ever repay for the laughter, wisdom, and love they have extended to me.

As you can see by now, Canada holds a very dear place in my heart. When I turned my attention to her folklore in preparation for writing this book, it was like learning a new side of a very close and personal friend. As I traveled the highways collecting stories, as I dug deeply into the archives in Ottawa reading old books, and as I delved into the history, the mythology, the legends, and the spooky tales from Prince Edward Island to Nunavut to the Yukon, I fell in love with Canada all over again. I found far more material than I could ever put into one book, so I chose to retell those stories that to me represented the special flavor of each province and its people. (And of course, I slipped in a few favorites along the way!)

So come, journey with me through one of my favorite places in the entire world. Read about the Nova Scotia forerunners, the Yukon Shangri-La, La Corriveau of Quebec, the Tammatuyuq of Nunavut, the Wendigo of the Northwest Territories, and many more wonderful tales that are part and parcel of the rich heritage of this great land. And next summer, if you happen to be fishing in Quebec, come stop by our campfire and share your story with me. I'll see you there!

— Sandy Schlosser

PART ONE
Ghost Stories

Black Bartelmy's Ghost

YARMOUTH, NOVA SCOTIA

Black Bartelmy was an evil, surly buccaneer who murdered his wife and children and went to sea with a band of pirates as nasty as he. He roamed the Atlantic coast, murdering and pillaging and laying waste to the countryside as he passed. By the time he approached Cape Forchu in Nova Scotia, Black Bartelmy had a ship loaded with treasure: a hull filled to overflowing with chests of gold and jewels and goblets and mighty swords.

A thick Fundy fog lay over the bay as the ship approached. The waves began to roil and thunder as the treacherous Fundy tide took hold of the evil man's ship. The crashing, churning waters of the Roaring Bull, that dangerous ledge of rocks near Cape Forchu, took the pirate's ship and smashed its hull to pieces. Seawater poured into the beleaguered ship, and it listed sideways, throwing most of the crew overboard to drown in the raging sea. Captain Bartelmy and a few other lucky sailors managed to grab the rail, as more of the men were swept overboard by a giant wave.

Captain Bartelmy pulled himself upright, cursing his ill-luck. Then his devilish black eyes spotted land to the starboard side of the ship. An evil smile lit his face, and he staggered toward his first mate, Ben the Hook, who was snapping orders to the six remaining sailors to lower the tenders into the water before more lives were lost. Here was Bartelmy's chance to escape without having to share the treasure, and he knew that Ben the Hook would help him.

The captain and Ben the Hook slipped into the rapidly filling hull and managed to slosh their way through knee-deep water and retrieve two treasure chests. Panting and swearing and staggering against the swaying ship, the men finally wrestled the two chests topside. Then the captain and his mate approached the remaining crew members, who were struggling to lower the tenders as the ship listed further and further to starboard. Drawing a knife from his belt, the captain stabbed first one then the other of the men standing at the front of the tender, while Ben slit the throats of two more with his hook. When the two remaining sailors realized what was happening, they put up a fight, but were quickly subdued and killed by the wily captain and his mate.

The ship groaned terribly as Black Bartelmy shoved the last body overboard. The captain and the mate hurriedly loaded the two chests onto one of the tenders and rowed as quickly as they could through the fog to avoid being caught in the sinking ship's wake as it slipped beneath the roiling waves.

After a long struggle against the terrible Fundy tide, the two men managed to reach the calmer waters of the cape. After searching for a place to bury their treasure, they found a large basalt cave and piled each chest inside. Then they covered the entrance with rocks.

As Ben the Hook rolled the last boulder into place, Black Bartelmy thrust a sword deep into his chest, twisted it with an evil laugh, and watched as the first mate fell dead at his feet. "Mine, all mine," the evil captain gloated, as he dug a shallow grave at the entrance to the cave for his erstwhile companion in crime. "Your ghost will guard the treasure for me," he added, kicking the body of the dead pirate down into the hole and covering it with dirt, sand, and stones.

Knowing that he had to leave this remote spot or starve, the evil pirate captain walked along the edge of the water, searching for a town or a harbor where he might row the tender. But all he found was fog and rain and howling wind and swamp. Roaring and cursing with rage, the dark captain stomped onward, careless of where his booted feet took him in the swirling mist. Then he took one last fatal step and found himself sinking into a quagmire. He was alone in this desolate place with no one to save him. Cursing his misfortune, he blasphemed all and committed his soul to Hades as his body sank down and down into the mire and was engulfed.

One stormy night soon after the pirate's death, the keeper of the local lighthouse saw a flare going up in the direction of the Roaring Bull. Thinking it was a ship in trouble, the keeper called together a lifeboat crew. Running into the roiling water, they launched their boat into the icy waves, heading for the Roaring Bull. But as they approached the vessel in distress, they saw a broken pirate's galleon with tattered, black sails listing against the terrible rocks. Then, before their eyes, the ship righted itself, the broken wood of its hull melting together to become whole, and the torn sails mending themselves. The

4

BLACK BARTELMY'S GHOST

ship began to glow from within, and before their dazed eyes, the rescuers saw that its decks were now piled high with treasure chests spilling over with gold.

Astride the deck stood a solitary man dressed in a black pirate captain's uniform. As the mariners gaped at him in astonishment, the ghost of Black Bartelmy grinned wickedly down at the men, gesturing grandly with his cutlass. Around the rescue boat, the wind began to swirl and the breakers rose as if possessed, lashing the craft again and again with their killing, chilly waters. The boat overturned, flinging the men into the raging sea, and the last thing the keeper and the rescuers heard was the sound of Black Bartelmy's ghost laughing. Only one man survived to bring a warning to the nearby villages of the ghost ship and its evil master.

To this day, the ghost of Black Bartelmy continues to haunt Cape Forchu and the Roaring Bull. Any rescue crew summoned to save a vessel off the Roaring Bull should take every precaution, because the distressed vessel might not really be there.

Ghost Train

MEDICINE HAT, ALBERTA

I was a railway fireman back in those days, working on the Canadian Pacific Railway line in Alberta. I did a hard day's work and earned a fair wage. I was young then. Me and my pretty little bride were just setting up housekeeping in a tiny cottage that was all we could afford on my starting salary. We were poor as church mice, Annie and me, but life was good and I was going to work my way right up to engineer one of these days and give Annie everything her heart desired.

Long about January of '08, the doc came for a visit to our little home, and over dinner he and a beaming Annie told me I was going to be a father. I just about fell out of my chair—a piece of pot roast still dangling from my fork—when I heard the news. After swallowing a few times, I felt myself start to smile so hard I thought my cheeks would burst from the strain. Me! A papa! I swooped Annie up and danced her about the room, until I remembered her fragile condition. Then I wanted to make her lie down for the next six months or so. How the doc and Annie did laugh at my antics.

I couldn't wait to get to work that night and tell my buddy

7

Twohey about the baby. Twohey was working the line as an engineer, and he'd taken me under his wing when I first signed onto the CPR line. He was nearly as excited as me when he heard the news.

"Barnaby, that's something!" Twohey shouted, pounding me on the back. "It'll be a boy! A bouncing boy just like his Pa!"

"Could be a girl," I warned him.

"Pretty as her Ma!" Twohey agreed at once. "You'll have to keep watch over her night and day or some fellow will steal her away!"

We laughed long and hard that day as I fired up the steam engine and Twohey drove her out of Medicine Hat and down the line. Oh, we had plans for this little one. Big plans. Twohey's ambitions for the child were even grander than mine. Twohey didn't have any kids of his own. His wife had found frontier life too harsh for her sensibilities and had gone back East, hoping Twohey would come to his senses and join her. She didn't have a prayer. Twohey was a wild frontiersman. If he weren't so crazy over machinery, Twohey would have made a fine cowboy, or maybe a gunslinger. Anyhow, he'd never leave the West to live in some tame, namby-pamby farming town in the East.

Well, the months passed quickly. Annie got as round as a ball, and I started getting a might nervous about all the hard work she was doing around our little cottage. I wanted her to rest, and she wanted to cook and clean and attend the sewing circle and do all the things the other community ladies did. Twohey and the other railmen told me I was as broody as a hen, but I didn't care. Only a few more months and I would be a papa for the first time, and this papa wanted to make sure mama was around to enjoy the new baby. I had the doc come out special to make sure everything was okay, and he chuckled and told me Annie was as healthy as a horse. In fact, she was healthier than me, since my nerves had caused me to lose weight. So *I* was the one put on a strict diet to help me gain back some pounds and calm my nerves. Twohey and Annie got a good laugh out of that one!

Two months left. I was nervously counting the days and was a bit concerned when the railroad asked me to take the night shift for the month of May. Annie grinned and told me to go ahead. She would be fine. The baby wasn't due yet, and if something came up during the night, the neighbor-lady lived right across the yard and would be listening for the sound of the cowbell that I had placed on the nightstand beside our bed. So I started my new shift, feeling somewhat reassured. Happily, Twohey had also taken the night shift, which helped a lot.

Along about the middle of the month, I found myself mounting the engine almost sick with dread. Something bad was going to happen to Annie. I was sure of it. Twohey was doing his best to reassure me on this point as we drove out of Medicine Hat that night. I was still shaky inside about three kilometers out of Medicine Hat when a blazing light appeared directly in front of the engine. It was another train on a collision course with us! Twohey yelled at me to jump, but there was no time. The light was right on top of us. I thought we were dead.

Then the oncoming train veered off to the right and ran past us, its whistle blowing and the passengers staring at us through the windows. But that was impossible! There was only a single track in that stretch, and it was the one we were on. I looked over at the shrieking, rumbling Ghost Train and saw that its wheels were not touching the ground!

Twohey braked our train, and when she came to a stop, we both bent double, breathing hard in fear and shock. We didn't start the train again until our shaking hands were under control.

"Wh . . . what was that?" I gasped to Twohey. He shook his head grimly, refusing to speak of the Ghost Train we'd seen.

"At least you know that premonition wasn't about Annie," he told me gruffly when we finished our shift. He went right in to the station master's office and requested some time off from engineering. He didn't say anything to me about it, but I knew he was shaken by the incident and wanted me to switch to yard work along with him. But I couldn't. It was less than two months until the baby was due, and I needed the pay badly. I kept working the night shift as a fireman, refusing to let the Ghost Train drive me away from a job that paid well and that I had always enjoyed.

Near the end of May, I was stoking the fire for an engineer named Nicholson when we heard a shrill whistle blast through the calm night air. We were on the exact same single track just outside of Medicine Hat when the brilliant light of the Ghost Train burst out of nowhere, blinding us. Nicholson gave a shout of terror, and I thought my heart would stop. As before,

GHOST TRAIN

the Ghost Train veered off to the right at the last possible second. I saw it race past us on tracks that did not exist, its passengers staring curiously at Nicholson and me from the windows.

That did it. I wasn't about to go back on the tracks after that, and Annie agreed with me. Better a poor, living papa for her baby than a rich, dead one. I did yard work for the rest of the month of May and a few weeks in June. No one reported any further Ghost Train sightings. Finally, I decided that enough was enough. I was a skilled fireman, and I was tired of skulking in the yard for fear of some ghost. Twohey had gone back to engineering at the beginning of June, and I followed his example about three weeks before the baby was due.

I was firing up an engine in the yard one evening, waiting tensely for a neighbor to come running up to tell me that Annie was in labor. The baby was a week overdue, not an uncommon occurrence, according to the doc, but it made me crazy. I was ready to faint with the strain, though Annie was still calm and blooming, even though she was rounder than a barrel and couldn't see her feet below her belly!

Suddenly there came a flurry of footsteps and the sound of an alarm. My first thought was of Annie; but no, this was a train accident. I flew with the others to hear the news. The *Spokane Flyer* and a Lethbridge passenger train had collided head-on on the single track three kilometers outside of Medicine Hat, on the exact spot where the Ghost Train had appeared. The Lethbridge locomotive had derailed, and its baggage car was destroyed. Seven people were killed in the accident, including the two engineers. One was my buddy

Twohey, and the other was Nicholson.

The boss took one look at my face when I heard about Twohey's death and sent me home for the night. I was shaking so badly I could hardly walk, and I was still trying to get a grip on my thoughts when my eyes registered a blaze of light coming from my cottage and the doc's carriage parked in front. The baby!

I went running for my door, my heart thundering in my chest. *I hope it's a boy,* I thought almost incoherently, my dead buddy's face rising before my eyes. *Please be a boy.*

I burst in the door, glanced frantically at my neighbor's wife, who was boiling a kettle on the stove. Then the bedroom door opened.

"Barnaby! Come in and meet your son," the doctor said happily.

I staggered inside, my eyes going straight to the bed. Annie—was Annie all right? And there she was, tired and achy and beaming with delight. She was holding a squirming bundle with a pert nose, a full head of red hair, and deep, wise eyes. The little infant frowned at me for a moment, and then wailed sharply.

"Is that any way to greet your Pa?" Annie scolded lovingly.

The doc pushed me into a chair before I fell over, and Annie thrust the wailing baby into my arms. I stared down at the little life, born as my dear friend departed his, and didn't know whether to laugh or cry. So I did both.

We named him Twohey.

3

The Dungarvon Whooper

DUNGARVON RIVER, NEW BRUNSWICK

Well, folks warned me about the Dungarvon Whooper as soon as I purchased land near the old logging camp by the river, but I didn't believe in ghosts and just laughed at their dire predictions. I was going to build a hunting lodge for me and my buddies so we'd have someplace to stay during fishing season, when the Atlantic salmon filled the Dungarvon River. And I was going to build it with my own two hands.

Folks in town were pretty incredulous when I told them my plans. One fellow even called me a city slicker. Guess he didn't like my shirt and tie. Probably wouldn't have believed me if I told him I'd grown up on a dirt-poor farm in northern Saskatchewan. If it hadn't been for my father's skills in hunting and trapping and fishing, we wouldn't have survived some of those terrible winters. After that upbringing, I found the Maritimes rather settled and overpopulated. Nearly as bad as the States. But beautiful in spite of the crowd, and you couldn't beat the salmon fishing on the Dungarvon.

It was early summer when I started my project. My father was an excellent carpenter—you had to be in the North

Country—and I learned everything I needed to know standing at his knee. I planned a rustic log cabin, and I spent my days sawing and measuring and hammering, as happy as a cricket in a haystack. I worked hard each day, leaving at dusk to make the long drive back to civilization and my rented apartment, where I would crash until dawn, sleeping the sleep of the truly exhausted. I had only two months to complete this particular project, and I was determined to finish in that time.

During the long summer days, I spent a lot of time thinking about the Dungarvon Whooper. According to my sources, there were two stories that were commonly used to explain it.

In the first story (which I considered a little tame), a giant logjam formed on the river early one spring, and the lumberjacks struggled and struggled to break it apart. The logs were overdue at the mill downstream, and with each day that passed the log pileup grew larger and harder to shift and more dangerous. Finally, a fellow named Dungarvon decided to tackle the problem all by his lonesome.

While his comrades watched in skepticism and fear, Dungarvon pushed and shoved at the logjam, balancing expertly atop the floating mass, until he removed a few key logs. Immediately, the water pressure from the spring floods began moving the whole pile. Dungarvon gave a whoop of triumph and joy as the logjam began to break up incredibly fast, logs practically flying through the air to freedom.

It was only then that Dungarvon realized that he was in danger. He dashed bravely from log to log, balancing and hopping and spinning on his feet with amazing dexterity, making for shore. But the break-up happened so swiftly that he was finally swept under the crashing, rolling logs that were smashing their way downriver toward the mill, and Dungarvon was killed.

Within a few weeks after the lumberman's death, people began reporting a strange whooping sound coming from the spot where the logjam had formed on the river. It occurred right at the place where Dungarvon was killed, and folks began saying it was his ghost haunting the banks of the river that caused his death.

The second story—the one I personally favored—went as follows. During one particularly cold winter sometime in the 1800s, a logging camp near the Dungarvon River stood waist deep in snow. The camp cook was a jolly fellow and handy with the spices, which made mealtime a posh occasion. The cook was rich for a logger, and he kept his life savings in a money belt that he wore at all times. The older lumberjacks considered him a bit of a fool for keeping so much money on his person, but that didn't discourage the cook one whit.

Now an Irish lumberjack named Ryan coveted the cook's money and concocted a plan to get it. He was the best hunter in camp, and he promised to teach the cook his secrets. The two men set off one Sunday on a hunting trip. When they were deep in the woods, Ryan swiftly turned his rifle on the cook and shot him dead. He unhooked the money belt off the body and began hacking his way through the snow and ice with a large stick he found nearby. About an hour later, he had managed single-handedly to bury the corpse under a combination of heavy snow and fallen branches.

When he returned to camp alone, Ryan told his fellow

loggers that they had been attacked by a bear. Ryan claimed to have been knocked out by a glancing blow and said that when he came to, he found that the cook had been dragged away. Ryan told the lumberjacks that he had tried to track the bear, but a short snow shower had obliterated the tracks. Search parties were sent out, but they found no trace of the dead cook. Meanwhile, Ryan trumped up an excuse and left the lumber camp for good while the men were out searching. No one ever saw him again.

At sundown that night, the lumberjacks heard a terrible screaming that seemed to come from everywhere at once—and yet from nowhere. The men recognized the voice as that of the cook. They searched desperately for the man as the screams grew louder and louder, but they could find no tracks in the snow save their own. After ten minutes, the screams stopped as abruptly as they had started.

The men searched again in the morning for the cook, but could find no trace of him. At dusk that night, the screams began again. The men were terrified and decided that it must be the ghost of the cook screaming in terror. By this time, they all knew that Ryan had left the camp, and the lumberjacks began to question the Irishman's story of the bear attack.

At dusk every evening for several weeks, the ghost of the cook shrieked out his terror and rage over his murder. All action in the logging camp ceased at the first sound of the "Dungarvon Whooper," as the ghost came to be called, and no one dared move until the sound died away. At the first sign of spring, the loggers packed up camp and hurried away.

The ghost was not heard so frequently after the camp was

THE DUNGARVON WHOOPER

disbanded, but local residents were still subjected every so often to the terrible screams of the Dungarvon Whooper. The ghost hung around the region for many years, and the residents finally called in a priest to lay the spirit to rest. The holy man prayed over the area and tried to exorcise the spirit with bell, book, and candle, but the ghost was too strong for him, and he left in defeat. From that day to this, the Dungarvon Whooper has continued to haunt the banks of the river. Or at least, that's the story as it was told me by the locals. I'd have a lot of fun relating it to my guests when I brought them to the lodge next summer.

In the meantime, I finished the exterior of the lodge and moved inside. Just in time too, because the days were turning cool and damp. I found myself dodging raindrops more often then not as I ran back and forth to my truck to grab plywood or lumber or supplies out of the back.

One morning, I threw my fishing tackle into the truck along with a couple of sleeping bags. I'd had enough of running back and forth to town each evening when I finished work. I was going to spend the night in my new lodge. I was expecting a buddy of mine to come up from Toronto to spend a few weeks helping me tidy things up as much as possible before cold weather hit (or my vacation time ran out—whichever came first), so I made up a spare "bedroom" for him in the lodge, complete with a sleeping bag, a pillow, some beef jerky, and written directions to the outhouse I'd constructed out back. What more could a fellow want?

I stopped work a mite earlier than usual on the day my buddy was due to arrive and headed down to the river to do some fishing. I found a good spot and settled down to battle with the fish. The river chuckled and gurgled and danced in its banks. The trees murmured to themselves in the end-of-summer breeze, and sunlight cast flickering shadows over the ground. I heard birds chirping and watched a couple of squirrels chase each other frantically up one side of a tree and down the other.

I felt my shoulders relax and grinned to myself, even though nary a bite was taken from my fly. This was the life! This was the reason I was building the hunting lodge. Peace and quiet and nature. A ray of sunlight lit the water, showing me a couple of Atlantic salmon who were completely ignoring my bait. Even that sight was beautiful.

The sky was aglow with the gold and coral and pink of sunset, and I was just wishing I had brought my jacket down to the river with me when the air was pierced with a terrible scream that seemed to come from directly behind me. I nearly jumped out of my skin and whirled around to see where the sound had come from, ready to flee if necessary. My heart was pounding so hard it hurt my chest, but my eyes beheld nothing. Then the hair-raising, high-pitched howl came again, this time from my right. It sounded as if someone were being tortured to death. I whirled again, but there was no one there. The eerie whooping sound came again a third time from the opposite bank of the river, and I dropped my pole—fly still floating on top of the water—and ran as fast as my feet would take me toward the lodge.

The air was filled from all sides with the terrible shrieking—the sound of a man's voice as he was horribly murdered for his money. Through the growing darkness, I saw a battered truck pull into the rough lane I had carved into the brush beside the lodge. For a moment I was almost blinded by headlights. Then my buddy Pete jumped out and came running toward me, shouting, "What is it? What's wrong? Who's screaming?"

I could barely hear him above the unearthly wails that rang through the clearing. I threw myself through the door of the lodge, barely keeping it open long enough for Pete to get in. Then I slammed it shut, jammed a two-by-four in front of it, and lit an old oil lamp with shaking hands.

"What was that sound? Is someone in trouble?" Pete was frantic with worry.

Outside, the screams slowly died away.

"That, my friend," I managed to say, after taking several calming breaths, "was the Dungarvon Whooper."

I would explain no further until we'd lit a fire in the fireplace and roasted up a couple of hot dogs for dinner. Pete was incredulous when I told him the story of the cook's ghost.

"Raccoons," he said at once. "Or a couple of the locals having you on. Take your pick."

Now that the horrible sound had faded away, I was inclined to believe him. At least enough to give it another go. So we settled in for the night, laughing at our foolishness. Over the next several days of hard work on the lodge, the matter became quite a joke to us.

Four days later, as dusk fell, the unearthly screaming began again. First on one side of the lodge, then down by the river, then in back of the lodge, and then all around us. The hair on my arms stood straight up, and my whole body shook with fright, for all that I pretended not to care. Pete and I took flashlights and ran from thicket to thicket, searching for the raccoons or prowlers who were trying to scare us. The final scream came right over our heads with such a blast of cold air that we both fell to our knees. As the heart-rending shriek died away, I flopped over on my side, curled into fetal position to try to calm my shaking body. At last I rose, my knees so weak I could hardly stand, and then pulled Pete to his feet. We stood in front of my new hunting lodge staring at one another mutely. We had uncovered nothing and no one during our frantic searching. It was obvious to both of us that we were alone. No one—at least no one visible—inhabited this place save ourselves.

That last thought was enough for me.

"Let's get out of here," I said. Pete nodded, speechless. We collected our things in record time and nearly spun out the trucks in our fervent desire to put as much distance as possible between ourselves and the Dungarvon Whooper.

Within a week, I'd sold the property to a *real* city slicker—one who didn't believe in ghosts—and Pete and I were headed back to Toronto. I'd find another place to build a hunting lodge. I was done with the Dungarvon River and its ghost.

4

Lost!

DAWSON CITY, YUKON

He'd spent many frustrating months in Dawson City, seeking to make his fortune in the Klondike gold fields. Thousands had stampeded to the Klondike, hoping to become one of the rags-to-riches miners hyped by the newspaper stories. But by the time the prospector arrived in town, the gold-bearing creeks had all been staked and speculators had claimed the rest.

The prospector hated Dawson City. It was a bawdy frontier town made out of wood and tents and filled to overflowing with dance halls, brothels, saloons, and newspapers. It had tons of gold, vats of whisky, reckless gamblers, scarlet women, and a riotous swirl of social activity. Even six sawmills running full time couldn't keep up with the demand Dawson City had for lumber. To the prospector's disgust, on his first day in town he was charged five dollars for a simple meal of beans, stewed apples, bread, and coffee. He could have paid fifteen cents for the same meal back home in Seattle.

Dawson was a city of contrasts. While the rich had champagne and caviar for breakfast, the unlucky poor had stale bread with lard and black coffee. Society matrons held lavish tea parties, while the indigent around them fell ill with scurvy, typhoid, and dysentery. Many perished; unable to afford the services of the Dawson City doctors, who charged $200 a visit.

Most of all, the prospector hated the heat and the mosquitoes, the mud, and the filth that filled the whole city with stench and disease. Horses got stuck in the muck of the streets, and wagons sank up to their axles. Pedestrians often had to wade knee-deep through a festering mass of putrid slime just to walk from one side of the street to another.

Disgusted, the prospector left the city and set out to explore on his own, hoping to find gold that had not already been claimed. His only companions on this dangerous journey were his two dogs, faithful creatures that he had raised from pups. Together, they wandered far in their search for wealth, until the prospector was beyond any place that looked familiar.

Normally, being lost in the Yukon wouldn't have trouble him. He could follow the stars at night, and sooner or later, if he kept going south, he figured he was bound to reach civilization. But the prospector had detected an early chill in the air that worried him. He was not equipped to be out alone during a Yukon winter, and the icy undertones he felt each night indicated that winter might come earlier than expected.

So the prospector and his dogs headed south, abandoning for the most part their search for gold in favor of finding civilization. He began rationing the food he carried in his pack, taking little time for hunting in order to keep up a steady, fast pace.

One evening as it neared dusk, he found himself mired down in the muskeg—a treacherous, boggy country with water hidden below the surface of the ground but above the deeper permafrost. The prospector knew that it would be all too easy to sink beneath the seemingly solid surface of the muskeg and drown in the hidden waters underneath. But the more the prospector and his dogs tried to free themselves from the bog's clutches, the more hopeless their situation became.

Just as the prospector resigned himself to spending the night in the bog, he caught a glimpse of a small game trail leading northward toward a pass in the mountains. It would take them the wrong way, away from civilization, but the prospector was desperate, so he followed the trail with his dogs, using a long walking stick to help him assess each potentially dangerous spot. He carefully stayed behind his dogs, which showed themselves fairly adept at locating places where a heavy body could break through the ground and slip into the hidden pools below.

Even with the game trail to aid them, it was tense and tiring work to navigate the muskeg, and the prospector knew that they needed to find a safe place to rest before darkness fell or exhaustion made them careless. He increased his pace slightly, and after another tense half hour, the ground under him firmed. His dogs barked excitedly and began running up the broadening trail toward the pass above them.

The prospector followed, relieved to be on safe ground at last. Within moments, he entered a narrow canyon pass through the mountain. Ahead of him, the dogs were barking feverishly in a manner that told him they had scented game. He quickened his pace, eager for fresh meat. As he did so, he became aware of a warm, balmy breeze more reminiscent of an island in the Caribbean than a mountain pass in the Yukon.

A moment later, to his surprise, he emerged into a lush green paradise. Below him opened a round valley several miles wide. It was cup-shaped and surrounded by ice-covered mountain peaks. The prospector figured it must have once been the bed of an ancient volcano. Around him he could smell sulfur and see steam rising from hot springs around the edges of the valley.

With an excited whoop, the prospector followed his ecstatic dogs through the waist-high grass filled with wildflowers, laughing as his companions sniffed out a rabbit trail and chased it down into the beautiful valley. He saw stands of timber growing throughout the valley, interrupted now and again by wide meadows. A small lake at the center of the valley was filled with ducks and geese. Browsing along the edge of the water were herds of caribou. And swooping above his head, chirping and feeding and calling out to one another, were birds of every color and description. The prospector even spotted a large brown bear wandering peacefully along the edge of the valley where the snowy peaks came down to meet the greenery below them.

After a few moments, his parka grew too hot, and he shrugged it off. As he reached the edge of the small lake, his dogs came to him, each carrying a dead rabbit. They presented the rabbits to him, and he accepted them with enthusiasm, praising the dogs mightily. As night fell, he chose a spot close to the water and built a small fire to cook up the meat for their evening meal. The dogs snapped up their share hungrily and then settled down to a deep sleep before the fire, putting aside the day's terrors and delights as if they had never been.

The prospector wished he could do the same. As the stars came out overhead, the man tried to find a comfortable place to sleep, knowing that in the morning, he would have to leave this Shangri-La and once again face the quagmire below. Much as he would love to linger in this enchanted place, winter was still coming quickly. Its deadly cold and snow would find its way even to this amazing valley, and alone there was no way he could survive. Dread for the morrow kept him awake late into the evening.

At last, the prospector fell into an uneasy doze. As he slept, he dreamt that a fierce native warrior was standing over him, threatening him with a spear.

"Why have you invaded this sacred valley?" the warrior demanded. "Leave at once or I will kill you!"

"I was lost in the muskeg," the prospector said in his dream. "I followed a game trail out and it led me to this place. If you show me the way through the muskeg, I will gladly leave."

The warrior frowned down at him. "I am the protector of this place and cannot forsake it. But I will summon a guide for you."

The warrior raised his arms toward the sky and called something in a tongue the prospector could not understand. Then he vanished.

The prospector was awakened by the sudden growling of his dogs. Sitting up, he beheld the glowing figure of a beautiful Native American woman standing at the top of the hill. He blinked in amazement and felt chills run up and down his body. The ghostly woman beckoned to him, and to his surprise, his dogs ceased their growling and ran up to her. They pranced around her like pups, and he felt his fear fade away.

Packing up his gear, the prospector made his way up the enchanted valley, breathing in the lovely smell of night-blooming flowers as he walked through the meadow, grasses brushing his thighs. He paused for a moment when he reached the top of the hill to look down on the lake, which gleamed as it reflected the million bright stars above it, trying to fix it forever in his memory. Then he turned to face the ghostly guide who would help him and his dogs find their way through the treacherous muskeg that barred the way to this Shangri-La.

The glowing woman smiled at him. Then she raised her arms in the same gesture used by the warrior in his dream and transformed into a beautiful snow-white hare. The radiant hare hopped slowly ahead of the prospector, leading him southward through the narrow canyon and down to the darkened muskeg.

The prospector drew as close to his supernatural guide as he dared once they reached the muskeg. He followed it closely, deviating neither left nor right from its path for fear of the treacherous ground around him. The dogs crowded close to his heels, making no attempt to rush ahead. They showed no interest in chasing the glowing hare that guided them, although earlier that day they had made a meal of its kin.

For several hours, the prospector and his dogs followed the gleaming animal through the twists and turns of the dark quagmire as the brilliant stars hung high above them and a sliver of a moon sank below the horizon in the west. Just before dawn, they reached solid ground. The dogs let out

LOST!

excited barks and raced ahead, yipping and running in circles in their joy. Behind them, the prospector looked around and knew where he was. A rough, muddy road lay before him, leading back toward Dawson City.

Ahead of him, the white hare became once more the beautiful, glowing figure of a woman. The dogs danced up to her, and she patted their heads. Then she offered the prospector a sweet smile and vanished as the first rays of the sun pierced the horizon.

The prospector nodded his thanks, his eyes stinging with

tears that he was too proud to shed. Then he shifted the pack on his shoulder, whistled for his dogs, and started walking toward Dawson City. He'd sell his mining equipment and head back home in the morning, he decided, as he strode down the road. If the native warrior and the ghost woman had thought his reckless skin worth saving, then he was going to get a steady job and prove them right. He smiled at his prancing dogs and thought that they would approve.

5

The Trapper's Ghost

CHURCHILL FALLS, LABRADOR

"Fool, fool, fool!"

He berated himself violently as he struggled to stay upright and moving against the fierce wind, the lashing snow, the terrible cold. "Fool!" he howled at himself, his words whipped away instantaneously by the driving wind.

The blizzard had sprung up from nowhere and caught him by surprise. And it shouldn't have. Not a bit. He knew the signs to look for. Everyone knew the signs: A cloud bank on the far horizon; a touch of humidity in the air; a dreadful stillness in which only a light breeze stirred the cold landscape; no sign of any bird or creature. It was the silence that heralded the approach of a terrible storm.

The signs had all been there as he tramped forth across the surreal, snowy landscape to check his traps. But he had been fooled by the strangely warm sun and the gentle touch of the breeze. His mind had been on his slowly dwindling cash reserves. He needed food, and he needed money for supplies, or else he might not survive this unusually long and hard Labrador winter. Two or three full traps would mean meat on the table and skins to sell. Please God, let there be at least one beaver or lynx or wolf in the traps, he had thought as he started out in the sharp, sparkling snow, his stomach growling in response to the thought.

And there *had* been a beaver, thank Providence. He felt it thumping in the bag at his side as he stumbled and fought and cursed the snow and ice accumulating on his frozen body. The wind roared around his shaking form, howling like a thousand banshees, making the branches whip and strike against him. He smacked right into a tree trunk, which brought his dazed mind back to consciousness for a moment—long enough to push away from the tree and keep going.

And he had to keep walking, keep moving. To lay down and sleep now meant death. And oh, how sleepy he felt. How hard it was to fight for life when the snow drove against him, seeping inside his clothes and icing up his eyelashes and hair. He was wet, he was freezing cold, his legs were shaking with the strain, and he was so tired. So tired . . .

He was barely conscious of tripping over a root and falling into the snow. Face down, barely able to breath against the icy crystals, he could hear a soft tap-tap-tap as the snow fell against his hat, his scarf, his coat. A pleasant sound that lulled him to sleep. The howling wind seemed soft and far away to his frigid ears. The world had narrowed to this one small snowbank, which was growing pleasantly warm. He slept.

He was shaken awake by a huge, rough hand on his shoulder.

"Come on, lad. This is no place to be," a gruff voice said in his ear. He was unable to move, helpless against the cold in

THE TRAPPER'S GHOST

his body. He felt himself lifted, tossed over a giant shoulder covered by layer upon layer of skins, and carried to a roughly hewn sleigh.

His dazed eyes, only half-open because of his frozen eyelashes, saw eight pure white huskies snapping eagerly at the driving snowflakes and dancing in their harness. The wind howled in anger at losing its victim as his rescuer tossed him into the back of the sleigh. He sank down and down through dried bear and caribou skins, settling atop a large wolf pelt as his rescuer piled the others over him until only the very tip of his nose was free.

He heard the man calling to his white huskies. The sleigh lurched once, and then they were away. He was more awake now and aware of his wet, frozen clothes, slowly thawing in this sheltered spot away from the cold and snow and wind. The pungent, musky-smelling bear and caribou skins above him were driving away the chill, and the soft wolf skin beneath him was more comfortable than his little cot in the small cabin he called home. After a moment, he allowed his eyes to droop shut, knowing it was safe now to sleep. He had been rescued.

He was awakened for the second time by the same rough hand on his shoulder. He stared blurrily up at a rugged, cruel face with a long, straggly beard, merciless black eyes, and a hooked nose worthy of a Roman emperor. His rescuer tossed him once again over a broad shoulder, commanded his dogs to stay, and carried him into a warm, well-lit room. Looking around, he recognized the local inn near his home. The innkeeper was already hurrying toward him, exclaiming in horror as his rescuer placed him gently on a chair by the door.

He was not quite sure what happened next. To his feverish, half-frozen brain, it seemed as if the large man straightened up, gave him a grave nod, and then vanished into thin air. Which was ridiculous. Except that he heard the innkeeper gasp and an amazed murmur sweep the room, coming from the townsfolk who had holed up to talk and drink and play checkers while the blizzard raged outside.

He must have lost consciousness then, because his next memory was of crisp, clean bed sheets and the gentle voice of the innkeeper's wife urging him to sit up and drink some soup. He clutched the spoon in shaking hands and gulped gratefully at the nourishing liquid as the innkeeper came up the stairs and bustled into the room.

"You had a close call, my friend," the innkeeper told him. "Eat up the soup and get some rest. The storm will be blowing for another two or three days at least."

But he couldn't rest, not with the mystery of his rescuer on his mind. Swallowing another spoonful, he put the bowl aside and asked the innkeeper about his rescuer. The innkeeper blinked in surprise, and then shut the bedroom door and pulled a chair up to the bed.

"You haven't heard, then, about the phantom trapper?" the innkeeper asked.

"Phantom trapper?" the woodsman gasped, remembering the strange way that the man had vanished before his eyes.

"Aye, lad. I've seen him before this, a couple of times. Always during a terrible blizzard, and always bringing me some poor soul who was caught out in the storm."

Picking up the soup bowl, the innkeeper handed it to

him and urged him to finish his meal while he told the following tale.

There once was a trapper who roamed the wilds of Labrador on a sleigh pulled by eight pure-white huskies. He was a tall man, dressed in layer upon layer of animal skins, and he drove his team with a terrible ferocity across the frozen tundra.

The trapper was a cruel man, and the people in the local towns didn't much care for him. When he came to a town, he would sell his skins and then drink away his money at the local tavern. When he wasn't drunk, the trapper assaulted the local women, picked fights with the hard-working townsmen, and tried to sell alcohol to the natives. After a few days of such behavior, the town constable would toss the trapper out on his ear. Then the trapper would resume his roaming and trapping until he came to another town.

No one knew exactly how the trapper met his fate. It was rumored that he went a little too far in his pursuit of a local innkeeper's fair wife and was shot to death by her disgruntled husband. Other folks said that he lived to an old age and died alone out on the trail. However he died, it swiftly became clear that death did not end the labors of the cruel trapper. Each winter, his ghost roamed the wilds of Labrador on a sleigh pulled by eight white huskies. It was said that his spirit was refused entry into heaven and so remained in Labrador, atoning for the many sins he committed during his lifetime by helping lost travelers find their way home.

"Yes, lad," the innkeeper concluded. "Many a weary soul has looked up from their frantic circling to see a large sleigh pulled by white dogs coming toward them. If they follow it, they are led to safety."

"In my case, I was manhandled to safety," the woodsman said after swallowing the last of the soup. "I was already sleeping in a snowdrift when the phantom trapper stopped for me!"

"It's a lucky thing you live in Labrador, my lad," the innkeeper added, taking the empty bowl from him and waving him back against the pillows to sleep. "If you'd been in Quebec or the territories, there'd have been no ghost to save you."

He nodded his head against the pillows, sleepy again. Yes, he had been very lucky. Saved by a phantom. On the edge of sleep, his last thought was that the phantom trapper must be well on his way to atonement after this day's work. Outside the window, he thought he heard the sharp, happy bark of a pure-white husky. Then he slept.

6

Who Calls?

He met her by chance one day while paddling his canoe down the river to his favorite hunting spot. She was lithe and fair with a proud tilt to her head and a glow in her eyes that set her apart from other women. She sang softly to herself as she gathered herbs near the riverbed, and the sound of her lovely voice was sweeter than any music he had ever heard.

The Cree warrior was taken with her instantly. He felt that he had to meet her at once, but he did not want to frighten her. He made a few awkward, splashing motions with his paddle to alert her to his presence. By the time he beached his canoe, she had moved to the edge of the trees and was watching him warily.

He called to her in his own tongue, hoping that she would understand. She ducked her head shyly, then glanced up, eyes filled with curiosity and mischief. Oh, this was a rare one, he thought, his heart pounding. She answered him cautiously in a voice with no accent. A maiden of his people, then. Perhaps from the next village?

His hands were shaking with nerves as he leapt awkwardly

from the canoe and almost fell. He flushed with shame, for he was normally as graceful as the girl herself. But his rapidly beating heart seemed to sap all the strength and agility from him, and he tripped over a root and nearly fell into a bush as he made his way to where the girl stood watching him.

Her face was calm, but he saw gentle laughter dancing in her lovely, golden eyes. He would have retreated in embarrassment if it hadn't been for the light blush on her cheeks that said she was as moved at the sight of him as he was by her.

Their first sentences were awkward, though the air between them seemed to buzz with a swirl of emotions. It was as if another, very intense conversation without words was going on, while on the surface he was simply asking her name and about her family. Trying in a much too obvious manner to find out if she was married already. He despised his lack of finesse, but in the presence of this tiny girl, his keen mind seemed to turn to jelly.

In spite of his awkwardness (or perhaps because it endeared him to her) the girl agreed to meet him again the next day. And the next. Within a month, he had paddled down to her village to meet her father. And in another fortnight, they were betrothed.

He had never felt so happy in his life. He had many duties to perform as a hunter and a leader in his village, which took up many hours of each day. These tasks cut deeply into the time he had to see his beloved. But it would not be much longer until she was living in the village with him, and they would never be parted again.

The thought was a cheering one, and he hummed to

himself the song she had been singing when they first met as he carefully repaired his wigwam, wanting it to be perfect for the day he brought home its new mistress. By the time he was finished, the light was failing. But he had been parted from his beloved for almost a week, and he did not wish to wait a moment longer to see her. He set out immediately, in spite of the growing darkness, determined to paddle his canoe through the night. There would be a place waiting for him in her parent's home, he knew, no matter how late he arrived.

The river sang softly to itself under the clear saffron sky as he set off into the fragrant night. He glanced up through the trees, identifying certain favorite stars and chanting softly to himself, his thoughts all of her, imaging what she would say and do when she saw all the improvements he had made to the wigwam where she would come as a bride.

Suddenly, he heard his named. He jerked back to awareness, halting his paddling and allowing the canoe to drift as he searched for the speaker.

"Who calls?" he asked in his native tongue, and then repeated the words in French: "*Qu'appelle?*"

There was no response.

Deciding that he had imagined the sound, he took up his paddle and continued down the dark, murmuring river. A few moments later, he heard his name spoken again. It came from everywhere, and yet from nowhere, and something about the sound reminded him of his beloved. But of course, she could not be here in this empty place along the river. She was at home with her family.

"Who calls?" he cried. "*Qu'appelle?*"

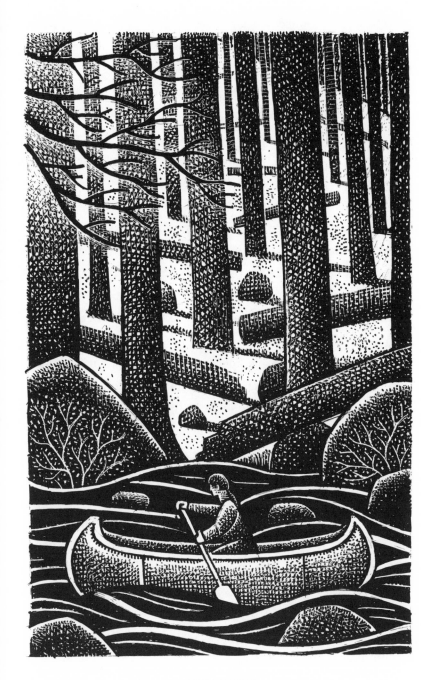

WHO CALLS?

His words bounced back to him from the surrounding valley, echoing and reverberating. The sound faded away and he listened intently, but there was no response.

The breeze swirled around him, touching his hair and his face. For a moment, the touch was that of his beloved, his fair one, and he closed his eyes and breathed deeply of the perfumed air. Almost, he thought he heard her voice in his ear, whispering his name. Then the breeze died away, and he took up his paddle and continued his journey to the home of his love.

He arrived at dawn and was met by his beloved's father. One look at the old warrior's face told him what had happened. His beloved, his fair one was gone. She had been taken with a high fever less than a day ago and had died during the night while he was journeying to her side. She had called his name twice, just before she breathed her last breath.

The warrior fell to his knees, weeping like a small child. Around him, the wind rose softly and swirled through his hair, across his cheek, as gentle as a touch. In his memory, he heard his beloved's voice calling to him in the night. He became aware at last of a strong hand gripping his shoulder and of tears other than his own falling against his ear as his beloved's father wept with him.

Finally he rose, took the old warrior's proffered arm, and stumbled to the family wigwam to weep again with the mother and help her prepare the body for burial. His beloved was gone. Oh, she was gone! And she had taken his heart with her. Grief-stricken and weak, the Cree warrior soon succumbed to the same fever that had taken his beloved and died within a fortnight.

But from that day to this, travelers on the river often hear the ghostly echo of the Cree warrior crying "*Qu'appelle?* Who calls?" as his spirit retraces that final journey downstream toward the home of his beloved.

7

Where's My Liver?

TORONTO, CANADA

"Go straight to the store and do not fool around," his mother said sternly as she handed over the money. "Your father is bringing home the boss tonight, and it's important that we make a good impression on him so he gives your father a raise."

Tommy nodded, trying to look serious and dependable through the dark mop of overlong hair that fell into his eyes. His father was always after him to get it cut.

"I'm serious, Tommy!" his mother said. "This is important. The boss's favorite meal is liver and onions. I want you to pick up the best liver they've got and bring it home right away. It's a holiday today, and the shops are closing early."

"I will, Ma," Tommy sulked. His mother had really been after him since he brought home a failing report card. Could he help it that the teachers didn't like him? At least the coach had given him good marks in gym.

Tommy stalked out of the kitchen, stuffing the money into the pocket of his pants, and grabbed his bicycle from the garage. He was nearly downtown when his friend Chad caught up with him and coasted his bike alongside. "Come on, Tommy!" Chad called. "The gang's playing baseball over at the park, and we need a pitcher."

Immediately, all thoughts of his errand fled from Tommy's mind. The two boys turned their bikes and headed toward the park. Tommy was hailed as a hero as soon as he arrived and was put up on the mound for the home team. Tommy was good— real good—and pitched a no-hitter to win the game for his team.

By the time the game ended, it was dark. As Chad and Tommy wheeled their bikes out of the park, Tommy remembered his errand. "The liver!" he gasped. "I've got to get to the store!"

Shouting goodbye to Chad, he leapt aboard his bike and rode as fast as he could to the local grocery. It was closed. All the local stores were shut up tight, and Tommy remembered too late that it was a holiday and the shops were scheduled to shut early.

"My mom's going to kill me," he gasped. First the bad report card, and now this! If he lost his father that raise, he would be grounded for life.

He wheeled his way slowly toward home, trying to come up with a plan or at least a good story. And then, as he rode past the cemetery, he got an idea. It was an awful idea, but it would save him from the even more awful fate that awaited him if he came home without a liver. His great-uncle had died a few days ago and had been buried in the cemetery. It had been a very cold spring, Tommy reasoned, and his liver was probably still fresh. What harm would it do to remove it? His uncle certainly didn't need it anymore.

With the thought came action. Tommy hurried home as silently as he could, slipped in the garage, got his father's shovel, and sharpened his jackknife. Five minutes later, he was back in the dark cemetery digging up his great-uncle's grave. And later that evening, his mother cooked up liver and onions for his father's boss and had actually thanked Tommy for helping her out.

The boss raved about the meal and had such a good time talking with Tommy's parents that he didn't leave until quite late. Tommy heaved a sigh of relief upon his exit and hurried up to his room to change for bed, happy to have gotten away with his ugly prank.

He fell asleep almost as soon as his head hit the pillow and was deep in dreamland when the wind outside the house began thrashing the tops of the trees as if in preparation for a thunderstorm. Yet the sky remained clear, and the moon shone its mysterious light through Tommy's window, casting eerie shadows on the carpet and walls.

"Where's my liver?" a sepulchral voice moaned softly from the street outside the house. "Where's my liver?"

Tommy turned over restlessly in his sleep but did not awaken. Moon shadows flickered across his neck like a noose, and a dark patch on the wall took on the shape of a bloody liver.

"Where's my liver?" a deep voice groaned from the front alcove. "Where's my liver?"

Tommy woke with a start and sat up in bed, sure that he had heard a voice. His pulse started pounding as his eyes frantically searched the shadows in his room. He heard something stirring downstairs, and the sound of heavy feet on the steps.

WHERE'S MY LIVER?

"Mom?" he called, his throat tight. "Dad? Is that you?"

But he knew it wasn't. He could hear his mother's dainty snore and his father's full-throated blast coming from the master bedroom at the end of the corridor.

"Where's my liver? Who's got my liver?" A ghostly voice rose up from the staircase, deep and guttural. The words ended in a terrible shriek that made Tommy's ragged hair stand on end. He gasped in fear and flung himself under the covers as the thud of heavy footsteps reached the top of the steps.

Thump. Thump. Thump. The footsteps drew nearer, until they reached Tommy's door. "Where's my liver? Who's got my liver?" the horrible voice asked from outside Tommy's closed door.

"Go away. Go away. Go away," Tommy whispered repeatedly, not daring to peek out from under his covers. A bright light was growing in his room, piercing the cotton covers and making his eyes water. His whole body trembled in terror as once more the voice asked, "Where's my liver? Who's got my liver?"

Sheer terror made him suddenly bold. Tommy threw back the covers and found the shriveled white face of his great-uncle right above him. "We ate your liver!" he shouted.

"I know you did, Tommy," the rotting corpse of his great-uncle said softly, stretching out his bony hands toward the boy's shaking body. Tommy screamed.

The next morning, Tommy's parents discovered their teenage son lying dead on top of his bed, a look of sheer horror upon his stricken face. His liver had been ripped right out of his body, but the autopsy proved that the boy had already died of fright before his liver was removed.

8

Not Next to Him!

We'd been sitting around the bar for hours, drinking a few beers and telling stories. Somehow or other the talk turned to ghosts, and a few of the fellows spun some pretty improbable tales, trying to spook the rest of us. We just laughed at their antics. None of us believed in ghosts.

My pal Bill was pretty quiet through the storytelling, and finally I elbowed him in the ribs and said: "What's wrong with you, Bill? Seen a ghost?"

The other fellows all laughed.

Bill shrugged. "Not me. But my cousins in Manitoba were haunted by a ghost a few years ago."

This startling statement was met by silence. Several of us exchanged looks, and then I said: "You can't stop now, Bill. Tell us the story!"

Bill took a sip of beer, thumped his foot absently against the side of the bar for a moment, and then told us the story about his cousin. For the purposes of the story, he called her "Kate," though that wasn't her real name.

Apparently, Kate was a very pretty girl in her youth, but

49

headstrong and cantankerous when aroused. She started seeing a hard-bitten backwoods fellow, and her parents raised some objections. Not a good idea, as it turned out, for Kate got stubborn and insisted on marrying the man, even though the two were an obvious mismatch.

The young couple quarreled all the time, and before you know it they had spent thirty years fighting and bickering and complaining. The whole family was scandalized by their behavior and secretly wondered why they stayed together. But Kate was too ornery to admit she had made a mistake, and it was her man who finally up and left her.

It wasn't too long after their separation that the backwoodsman died and was quietly buried in the family plot, since he had no kin of his own. Kate put on black and went through the widow-routine good and proper, but she didn't shed many tears over her dead husband. She was still too angry at him for ruining her life. Never would admit that she was partially to blame.

Kate passed on about six years after her man and was buried next to him in the family plot. And that was when the trouble began. Two or three nights after the burial, Bill's cousin "Jack" was awakened by a bright light shining over his bed. He turned over and stared straight up into the shining white face of his cousin Kate. The ghost was hovering over the foot of the bed with folded arms and was tapping one toe against the air.

"Jack!" she bellowed, waking his sleeping wife. "Why in tarnation did you bury me next to *him*? I spent thirty years sleeping next to him, and I don't aim to spend the rest of

NOT NEXT TO HIM!

eternity at his side! You put me someplace else."

Jack's wife sat straight up in bed, stared at the ghost, and screamed so loudly that cousin Kate covered her ears with her hands.

"Good grief, woman, it's just me," she snapped at her cousin-in-law, and then faded away, leaving Jack and his wife in darkness.

"Eee! Ahh! Ohh!" Jack's wife gasped, unable to form a single word. She wrung her hands and then leapt out of bed to bounce up and down on the floor in intense agitation. "Eee! Ahh! Ohh!" she cried.

"I know what you mean," Jack said kindly from the bed. "Cousin Kate always had that effect on me, too, even when she was alive."

"Wh . . . what are we going to do?" his wife asked, regaining her voice after several false starts.

"Danged if I know!" Jack said. "Trust Kate to be a pest, even after death. Now come to bed before you catch cold!"

Jack's wife nodded obediently and slipped back under the covers. But her sleep was restless, and she woke with dark circles around her eyes. The rest of the family noticed it, and Jack's wife was quick to tell the tale. No one believed her at first. Said it was a nightmare brought on by all the heavy food she and Jack regularly consumed for their supper.

Then Kate's ghost appeared to her uncle and aunt, berating them in the same manner she had used with Jack and his wife. Next she appeared to her siblings, and then to some more cousins. Not one night passed without Kate's specter appearing to someone in the family, complaining bitterly because they'd laid her to rest next to *him*. She never said her husband's name, but they all knew to whom she referred.

About a month after the manifestation began, Kate's ghost reappeared in Jack's bedroom around midnight. Once again, Jack was awakened by a bright light in his eyes, and he sat straight up in bed, knowing what he was going to see. Yes, there was Kate, shining white and mad as all get-out, her arms folded across her ample chest and her toe tapping.

"I'm still next to *him!*" she said accusingly. "I thought I told you to move my body, Cousin Jack. I appeared to you first because you've always been the most reliable person in this family, and now you've let me down."

Jack's wife sat up, rubbing her eyes. "Lay off him, Kate," she told the angry specter. "We'll talk to the authorities in the morning and see about getting you exhumed. It's not like we're living a few centuries ago when all we'd have to do was dig you up and plop you down somewhere else."

"Well, get crackin'" Kate snapped and vanished with a pop.

"Gracious! Not even a thank-you," said Jack's wife. Jack chuckled and gave her a kiss, and they snuggled down together among the pillows to sleep.

The next day, the whole family went to both the civil authorities and the local church to tell their story. They were met with some skepticism and a lot of debate, but the earnestness of their pleas (and the fact that they threatened to sic the ghost of Kate on the local minister if he didn't listen to reason) won the day, and permission was given for them to exhume the body and move Kate to a more salubrious location.

The move was done quickly, but the family was careful to

observe enough pomp and ceremony to satisfy their demanding relative. None of them wanted Kate returning to scold them for lack of respect.

The family waited tensely for several weeks after the reburial, but Kate's ghost didn't appear. "Not even to say 'thank-you,'" Jack's wife said indignantly to her husband.

"Darling, just be glad she's gone," Jack told his wife. And everyone in the family agreed with him.

At the close of his story, Bill paused and took another sip of beer.

"Was the ghost of Kate ever seen again?" I asked.

Bill shook his head. "Not a peep out of her. Apparently, having got what she came back for, she was able to pass on to glory. And not a moment too soon, according to my cousin Jack."

Everyone at the bar nodded in agreement, and Bill's ghost story was voted the best of the evening. Then the bartender signaled last call, and our nightly storytelling session concluded with one more beer before we hit the road.

An Invitation to the Wedding

DAUPHIN, MANITOBA

There once were two friends living in Manitoba many years ago named Oleksander and Marko who went into business together running a small farm. They worked hard from dawn until dusk and stuck together through thick and thin, good times and bad, until they'd made a success of the farm.

They were young men in need of wives, and as soon as their farm had prospered and they had built themselves two nice houses down the lane from each other, they began eyeing all the pretty girls in town. Marko soon fell to the charms of the fair Eva and started courting her with long walks and bouquets of wild roses. Oleksander favored Lilia, who reminded him of his favorite flower.

"You must invite me to your wedding, Marko," Oleksander said one day as they were working in the field.

Marko was surprised by his words. "But of course, my friend. You will be my best man."

Oleksander looked up from his scything with a strange, faraway look in his eyes. "No, my friend. Another will have that honor in my place. But do not forget me. And tell your Eva to look after my Lilia, for she will miss me."

Marko was shocked by his friend's words and the strange, prophetic tone in his voice.

"Do not talk nonsense," he scolded, afraid to listen to his friend. But Oleksander was insistent that he promise to invite him to his wedding, and so Marko solemnly swore that he would.

Oleksander died in his sleep that night. The doctor said his heart had given out—and it took him so quickly he never awoke. Marko was heartbroken, and little Lilia would not stop weeping for days.

Oleksander's sudden death acted as a spur to Marko, convincing him that life was short and that he needed to act quickly to ensure his own happiness while he still had his health. Within a week he had proposed to his lovely Eva and was accepted. Eva's older brother, a sour man whom Marko did not like, was appointed to be his best man.

As was the custom, the two men went from house to house, bidding everyone in town to come to the wedding. At last, the whole town had received a personal invitation to the celebration from the mouth of the groom. All except for one man.

"I must invite my friend Oleksander to my wedding," Marko told his best man. "I promised him that I would."

Eva's brother eyed him with scorn. "That is ridiculous. Oleksander is dead," he said, and refused to accompany Marko to the cemetery.

So Marko went alone to the graveyard and stood in silence for a long time in front of his friend's tomb. Then he bowed low, and said: "I am sorry, my dear friend, that I come to you alone. My best man would not accompany me to your home, as was his duty. But *I* am here, and I beg that you will come to my wedding, for Eva and I will not count it as blessed unless you are there."

Marko bowed once more, tears running down his cheeks. Gruffly, he rubbed them away, and for a moment, the wind swirled around his face and hair, and in it he caught the faint sound of a chuckle that reminded him of Oleksander. Comforted, Marko left the cemetery and went to the home of his beloved to tell her that all the invitations had been given and that they could be married on the following Saturday.

The day of the wedding dawned crystal clear and warm. The whole town turned out for the ceremony, and the reception was held in the meadow next to the church. There was singing and dancing. One by one, the guests stepped forward and laid their gifts on the long table set in front of the bride and her groom.

Then, from the rear of the line, there came a startled murmur. It swept through the crowd, which parted slowly. Everyone stared at the tall figure walking slowly through the field. He was dressed all in white and carried a cane, which he used to nudge a few unnoticing folks out of his way. Under one arm he carried a lovely carved wooden chest.

Eva gasped and her fingers tightened within Marko's grasp until she nearly cut off the circulation. But Marko didn't notice. He was too busy staring at the ghost of Oleksander as his friend and partner strolled leisurely across the field. The guests made way for the tall spirit, who came right up to the table. Oleksander bowed to Marko and then to Eva. He laid the carved chest on the table, which sagged instantly under its weight.

"God's blessing be upon your marriage," Oleksander said quietly.

"Thank you, my friend," Marko replied, his voice choked with emotion.

Oleksander turned then, and the guests backed away from him in fear and awe. All except for little Lilia, who stood her ground, tears running down her cheeks. Oleksander walked up to her and took her hand in his. He leaned down and spoke a word or two in her ear. Then, as abruptly as he had arrived, he vanished.

Eva glanced from Marko to the chest and then back at her groom. He nodded and asked her to open it, for his hands were shaking too much to do it himself. Eva lifted the lid to reveal a pile of shining silver coins heaped inside. A small fortune. All the guests gasped in amazement. Marko was overcome by what had happened, and walked into the church to collect his thoughts. He was joined by Eva, who had left her parents in charge of the box of money so that she could come and comfort her groom.

Marko and Eva settled into the grand house he had built with his own two hands, and they asked Lilia, her brother, and her widowed mother to live in Oleksander's house down the lane. Marko and Lilia's brother ran the farm together with the help of the womenfolk.

Lilia's anguish had abated after Marko's wedding day. She was not as lighthearted as she once had been, but she grew

AN INVITATION TO THE WEDDING

rosy and plump and sometimes essayed a laugh at one of her brother's jokes. She never told anyone what Oleksander's ghost had said to her on Marko's wedding day, but it had obviously helped mute her terrible grief.

A few months after the wedding, Eva's brother announced his plans to wed a wealthy local girl. He asked Marko to be his best man, and the two men walked the town together, their roles reversed, to invite everyone to the wedding. When they had finished their task, Eva's brother announced that he was going to invite Oleksander to his wedding.

Marko raised his eyebrows in shock. Eva's brother had never liked Oleksander, and he had expressed his disapproval most assuredly the day he had refused to accompany Marko to the graveyard. This sudden change of heart probably had more to do with the chest full of silver than with any friendship felt for Oleksander, Marko thought. Marko did not approve of such greed, but he knew his duty, and so he accompanied Eva's brother to the cemetery to stand with him in front of his friend's grave.

As Eva's brother bowed to the tombstone, a violent wind sprang up, lashing the trees branches and whipping through the tall grass. Suddenly Oleksander appeared before them and drove his fist into the stomach of the prospective bridegroom, knocking him to the ground.

"You would not do your duty as best man to my friend Marko," the ghost roared in anger. "Yet now you dare to come here and invite me to your wedding, foolish one?"

Eva's brother gave a yelp of fear and fled from the cemetery without looking back. As he disappeared down the lane, the wind died away, and the air became still. Oleksander turned then to Marko and smiled ruefully.

"Thank you for looking after my Lilia," he said quietly. "May God bless you, my friend."

Then the ghost was gone, and Marko was alone in the cemetery.

Eva's brother made the mistake of confiding the tale of his ghostly encounter to a neighbor, who spread it all over town. When the day of the wedding came, only his closest relatives came to the ceremony and the reception that followed. The townsfolk were afraid to attend, fearing that Oleksander's ghost would punish them if they did.

Marko and Eva lived a long and prosperous life and had many children. After mourning Oleksander for five years, Lilia married a very nice older man who had recently moved into their town. Her husband came to work on the farm with Marko and Lilia's brother.

Oleksander's ghost was seen no more, though he was never forgotten, and Marko's eldest son bore his name.

La Corriveau

Surely, *mon ami*, you have heard the story of La Corriveau, *non*? Ah, but I forget that you are new to Quebec. Come then, let me tell you the tale.

Like many good stories, it begins with a beautiful but ruthless woman named Marie-Josephte Corriveau. A heartless girl she was, and headstrong. She married a good-looking man but soon grew bored with him and cast her eyes upon another. When the moment was ripe, she crept up on her husband, stunned him with a blow to the side of the head, and then took a whip to his horse, which trampled him to death. Or so they say. At the time, the death was ruled an accident, and La Corriveau was free to pursue her new love interest.

A few months passed, and La Corriveau was once again a bride. She was happy with her new love at first. But her heart was fickle, and she cast her eyes afield once more when her new man did not please her as well as she expected. Ah, *oui!* It is true. A third husband she desired to have—the man a handsome newcomer with the courtly manners of the Old World. But first she must be rid of her second husband.

Many claim she heated a pan full of lead on the stove one night and poured it into the ears of her sleeping husband. *Moi,* I think she did him in with an axe. Whatever the case, it was quickly obvious to all that the second husband's death was no accident. And La Corriveau—that heartless woman—she framed her father for the deed. He was taken to trial and found guilty of murder. Poor man, he loved his daughter and covered for her as long as he could, but he broke in the final moments before they hanged him, *oui,* and he told the magistrate the truth about his son-in-law's death.

La Corriveau was caught this time and put on trial. There was no mercy for such a one as she, and the rope was soon around her fair neck. When she was dead, they strung up her corpse in a large cage and hung it in a prominent place beside the main road along the river, where the good people of the city could watch it wither away and rot, proclaiming to all who saw her the price that was exacted for murder so foul.

Ah, but what the authorities did not guess, *mon ami,* was that the spirit of this evil woman would not die as it should. No. It was tied to her shackled, withering flesh. At night, the rotting eyes of the cadaver would open of their own accord, red flames glowing in their putrid depths. Desiccated hands that were more bone then flesh would reach toward those who passed her cage with a soft clanking of the chains that bound them. La Corriveau would whisper the travelers' names through a tangle of stringy locks. One look at the shriveled blue features and glowing red eyes was enough to send even the bravest souls fleeing as fast as their legs could carry them.

Soon, no one would use the river road after dark, preferring to go a mile out of the way rather than pass that evil place. So the authorities, they took the cage down and buried it deep beneath the ground, hoping that interment would silence the evil creature. But their hopes, they were in vain; for many a night, when the moon was dark and the wind was chill, the desiccated carcass of a woman, her cheeks withered and blue, her tight skin brown from long exposure to the sun, her hands rotting and bony where the dried flesh had flaked away, would walk back and forth along the river road, accosting night travelers.

This went on for more than a year. Then one night, a prominent citizen named Dubé was walking home along the river road after having a few drinks at the local tavern with *les amis.* Under his arm he carried a bottle of rum that he planned to share with his new bride over an intimate dinner. But as he passed the place where the cage of La Corriveau once stood, his eye was caught by a blue light flickering on the island across the river. He paused, pulse pounding with fear as the sound of wicked chanting drifted toward him through the darkness. He could see wild, demonic figures dancing around the blue light, and the name they were calling out was his own.

"*Madre de Dios,*" he gasped in fear—and then he screamed as a pair of bony, withered hands clutched his throat from behind.

"Take me across the river, Dubé," La Corriveau whispered into his ear, her rank breath and what was left of her greasy hair caressing his cheek. He flinched away from the slimy feel of the creature's locks on his skin and tried desperately to break the stranglehold the evil creature had on his neck. His skin crawled at the proximity of this horror, and he broke out in a cold

LA CORRIVEAU

sweat as he struggled in vain to break her grip.

"Take me across the river to the Devil's dance, Dubé," La Corriveau said again. "I cannot pass the blessed waters of the Saint Lawrence unless a Christian man carries me."

Fear leant Dubé a strength he did not normally possess. He dropped to his knees, ripping at the creature's hands and flinching as he felt dry flesh tearing away from La Corriveau's bones. Then he was free and rolling aside to avoid a kick from the hag-woman's rotting foot.

"In the name of the blessed Saint Anne and *la Madre de Dios,* leave me," Dubé shrieked as the wicked thing that had once been a woman bent over his prone form. Then he fainted and knew no more until the morning, when his frantic wife fell on her knees beside her new husband's body, sobbing frantically in fear that he had been killed by the evil machinations of La Corriveau.

The story of Dubé's attack spread through the city, and the authorities were forced to call in the holy *Curés* to exorcise the foul spirit and free the citizens from her evil spells.

Did the prayers of *les Curés* drive away La Corriveau? Who can say? There were no more official reports filed with the authorities, but people continued to tell stories about the creature long after Dubé and all of his generation had passed away.

And so, that is the tale of La Corriveau. A good story, *non?* And true, *oui,* at least in part, for Marie-Josephte Corriveau was a real woman who was hung right here in Quebec in April of 1763 for killing her husband. Check the records for yourself if you do not believe me. As for the rest of the tale, I leave it for you, *mon ami,* to decide what is fact, and what is fiction.

The Lady in White

TRACADIE-SHEILA, NEW BRUNSWICK

They'd taken the three-mast, thirty-foot fishing boat far off shore that day, since the fish weren't biting where they normally sailed. The wind and waves were calm—too calm, really, though neither father nor son took much notice of this as the sun set slowly into the west and darkness fell.

At first, the darkness covered the approach of the storm. A few cool puffs of wind were the only warning they had before the tempest blew down upon their small vessel. "We'd best make for shore, son," the father shouted above the roar of the wind and waves. Soaking wet and chilled to the bone, the boy could only nod as he raced to adjust the rigging while his father took the wheel.

The boat climbed up mountainous waves and then sank into the troughs behind them, only to begin another treacherous climb. They were buffeted from side to side constantly as the wind howled and shook the rigging; the sails were twisting and turning and flapping in a hissing, spitting fury as the rain poured down and the waves slopped water over the sides of the boat.

It was slow, heavy going in the storm. One hour passed, then two.

"Pa. Pa!" the son finally shouted over the wind. "Where's the light? We should be seeing the Tracadie light by now."

"I know!" the father yelled back from the wheel, his face grim. That was when the boy realized that they were lost. Lost at sea in a terrible storm. Who knew where they would blow to? And it was so dark and foggy and the waves were so high that they'd never be able to see a reef until it was too late. The boy drew in several shaky breaths, trying to stay calm.

All at once, a brilliant white light pierced through the storm. "The lighthouse," gasped the boy. But it wasn't the lighthouse. Ahead of the boat, a ball of light was gradually twisting into the shape of a bent old woman dressed all in white. She was holding a lantern that gave off a glow only a tad brighter than her body. One leg was shorter than the other, so her whole body canted a bit to the right.

Aboard the fishing vessel, father and son stared at the figure, and she stared back at them. Then the old woman turned and slowly began walking forward, heading to the left. After a moment's hesitation at the wheel, the father turned the vessel to follow her.

A sail started flapping wildly above them, recalling the boy to his duties. He rushed forward and corrected it, then turned his wondering eyes to the front of the boat, wiping the rain away from his lashes so he could better observe the little old lady all in white who was walking determinedly through the raging storm, her feet only a few inches above the terrible, roiling waves.

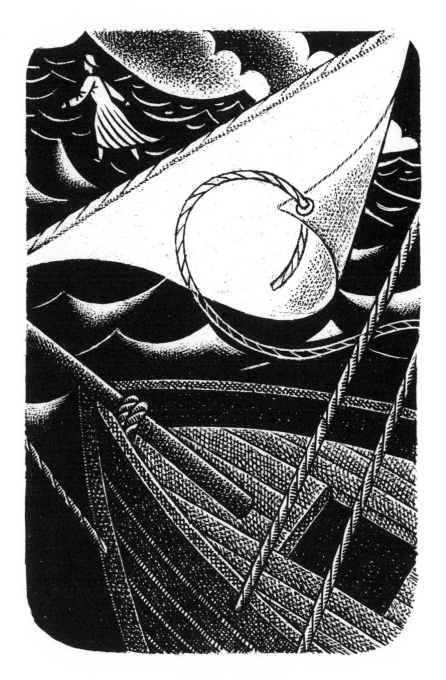

THE LADY IN WHITE

Time was meaningless in the thundering wind, whipping rain, and surging sea. The boy never knew how long it was that they followed the white lady through the storm. His actions became automatic as he grew more and more tired. But he kept working the sails as his father steered the boat first left, then right, and then left again, zigzagging in the wake of the woman in white.

Suddenly, as quickly as she had appeared, she was gone, leaving them alone in the roaring darkness. Father and son gasped in shock when she disappeared. And then, through the heavy rain, across the boiling sea, there came a flash of light from the Tracadie lighthouse, and they knew they were almost home.

It was well after midnight when they stumbled into their house to be met by the frantic wife-and-mother who had been anxiously waiting for them to return. She fell upon her men with tears and happy scolding, pulling them to the fire and wrapping them in blankets to warm them.

Haltingly, they told her about the lady in white who had guided them through the storm. The mother's eyes grew large with astonishment, and then she asked them to describe the lady with the lantern. When they did, she hurried out of the kitchen, and they heard her rummaging in the bedroom. She returned a moment later with a faded old picture in her hand.

Father and son gasped when they saw the photograph, recognizing the lady in white who had come to them in the storm. Smiling at them teary-eyed, the wife said simply: "This is a picture of my grandmother, for whom I was named. She died when I was ten years old."

The spirit of the frail old lady had come to save her granddaughter's husband and son and guide them safely to land during the terrible storm. "She saved our lives," the husband said shakily, and his wife nodded and kissed him, unable to speak. Then she pulled away from her man, ruffled her son's wet hair, and told them both to get upstairs to bed before they caught pneumonia and undid all of her granny's work.

Chuckling a little tremulously, they obeyed.

12

The Pitchfork

It was a cold, misty day in late October, and the townsmen hurried through their evening chores so they could gather around the pot-belly stove in the country store to warm themselves and swap stories. It was a perfect night for it: drippy and cold and miserable. No one in their right mind would want to be outside on such a dreary evening.

The talk was all of the harvest and speculations on the fierceness of the coming winter as Peter McIntyre swept into the store, shaking rain off his coat sleeves and calling a cheerful greeting to his friends in his broad Scottish accent. McIntyre was a fairly new settler to Prince Edward Island, having arrived on the *Alexander* in 1773.

McIntyre pulled up a chair and sat next to the warm stove as Ben Peters brought the conversation around to the strange light he'd seen several nights in a row out by the graveyard.

"It was huge," Ben exclaimed, his eyes popping out in his excitement. He threw his arms wide, almost knocking McIntyre in the head. "Big as a barn door. It danced across the graveyard, bobbing up and down on top of the stones as if it were being knocked to and fro by unearthly blasts of spirit air! The whole cemetery was lit up as if it were noonday."

"'Tis nonsense you're speaking!" McIntyre exclaimed crossly. "There's no such thing as ghosts, Ben Peters!"

"And I'm telling you I saw it. A huge light. It's the ghost of that unnamed fellow they put in the graveyard a few years back—the one that swept ashore after the storm. Folks say he was a pirate that sold his soul to the devil in exchange for gold!"

McIntyre grunted in disagreement, but everyone else around the stove nodded.

"You won't catch me anywhere near that graveyard after dark," Ben concluded.

This statement was too much for McIntyre. "'Tis a bunch of cowards you are behavin' like, to my mind," McIntyre sneered, folding his arms and leaning back in his chair in a superior fashion calculated to show his contempt. "You are exaggerating as usual, Ben Peters. Such nonsense will never keep *me* from walking through the cemetery. There are more devils among the lot of you than are out there in the graveyard, I be thinking."

"Well, then, why don't you take a stroll through the cemetery tonight, Peter McIntyre," Ben Peters dared him, upset at being called a coward.

"Yes, McIntyre," another fellow chimed in. "It's all well and good you putting on a brave front when you're here by the warm fire. But it's another thing to walk through a haunted cemetery in the dead of night all by yourself. You must be out of your mind to make such a boast!"

"Dead man's bones," intoned the blacksmith solemnly.

"Dead man's bones and their restless spirits."

"Superstitious nonsense," sputtered McIntyre, whose ire was up.

Irked by his superior attitude, the townsmen dared McIntyre to go to the cemetery that very night with a pitchfork and plant it in the center of the stranger's grave to prove he had been there. If the pitchfork was there in the morning, the townsmen would all chip in to buy him a pound of tobacco. If it wasn't, McIntyre would apologize for calling them cowards.

McIntyre accepted the bet immediately and swaggered to his feet as the shopkeeper was dispatched to get a pitchfork from his shed. "Better have that tobacco ready," he told his comrades. "I will not be detained overlong by dead spirits on this evening."

"That's what you think," muttered Ben Peters, glaring at the Scotsman.

McIntyre just laughed. "I've never known dead men to harm anyone," he said.

The shopkeeper came into the room with the pitchfork, and McIntyre took it with a flourish. He headed out into the dripping darkness, followed by his fellow townsmen, who waved him off on his journey and then scuttled home through the mist, trying to avoid the raindrops that were steadily growing heavier.

McIntyre whistled happily to himself as he walked quickly toward the cemetery. The thrifty Scot liked to smoke a pipe but wasn't always willing to pay the outrageous price the shopkeeper was charging for tobacco these days. Getting a pound of free tobacco would be a real treat.

So musing, he made his way through the rainy night, hugging his black slicker around him for warmth. The air grew colder by several degrees as he approached the dark cemetery in the woods, and McIntyre began to shiver in earnest. What a foul night to be out, he thought, clutching the pitchfork in hands that were shaking with cold. But the thought of that pound of tobacco—so easily won—drove him onward down the narrow footpath through the wet woods toward the cemetery.

It was so dark in the forest that he could barely see where he was going. McIntyre tripped over roots and rocks, cursing each time he stumbled. He nearly lost the pitchfork once and almost stabbed himself in the eye a second time when he ran into an inconveniently placed sapling near the entrance to the clearing.

Cursing aloud, he pushed his way past the erring tree and into the open area, which was only slightly less dark in the heavy cloud cover and the rain. McIntyre's hands were numb with cold as he made his way toward the center of the cemetery where the stranger's grave lay. He cursed the darkness aloud, and as he did so, his ears picked up a faint chuckle coming from behind him.

A cold shudder ran across his arms and legs as he whirled to face the sound. "Is that you, Ben Peters?" he demanded, holding the pitchfork in front of him like a weapon. But no one was there.

The harsh laugh came again from behind him. McIntyre whirled, thrusting the pitchfork out like a sword. Again, he saw no one. But the temperature dropped so suddenly he could feel the change, and a few of the raindrops turned to snow as they reached the air around the stranger's grave.

"Who are you?" McIntyre said, his voice quavering a bit in spite of the bold front he was putting on.

"Who are *you?*" countered the voice. Around McIntyre, the cemetery was gradually growing lighter. McIntyre whirled for a third time in the direction of the voice and saw a ball of pure blue light hovering over the grave of the drowned stranger. "And why have you come here?"

McIntyre opened and closed his mouth, but no words came out as the blue light slowly took the shape of an incredibly tall, too-thin phantom with a scraggly beard, a patch over one eye, and a cutlass at his waist. The phantom loomed over the Scotsman, his face transforming suddenly with rage: "You've come to steal my treasure!" he roared.

McIntyre screamed and dropped the pitchfork. Immediately, the phantom swooped down upon it. McIntyre turned and ran forward as fast as his shaking legs would carry him. But he tripped over a broken gravestone and fell heavily across the drowned man's tomb. He started to turn over and saw the phantom right above him, the pitchfork poised to strike.

McIntyre screamed as the pitchfork stabbed downward toward his torso. He felt a horrible pain in his head as if a blood vessel had burst inside his skull. Then the world went black.

Ben Peters was expecting McIntyre to show up on his doorstep at dawn to demand his tobacco, but the Scotsman did not come. Curious, he went to hunt down a few of his

THE PITCHFORK

cronies from the previous evening, and together they went searching for McIntyre to see how he had fared at the haunted cemetery. But his cabin was empty when they got there, and his bed hadn't been slept in.

Apprehensive now, the townsmen slowly made their way through the narrow footpath toward the graveyard, joking in overloud voices to cover their growing sense that something was amiss.

When they reached the cemetery clearing, the men saw the handle of a pitchfork showing above the gravestones.

"Glory be, he did it!" exclaimed Ben Peters. Then he looked closer, gasped, and hurried toward the grave at the center of the cemetery. A dark figure lay huddled on the ground under the pitchfork.

"Peter! Peter McIntyre! Can you hear me?" he cried, and the other men echoed him. Ben stopped abruptly a few yards from the huddled form. His followers nearly knocked him over, so sudden was his halt. Then they caught a glimpse of the body and stopped their forward rush. McIntyre's corpse lay with its face turned toward them, and the look of utter horror on his countenance would haunt their nightmares for the rest of their days.

Slowly, Ben moved forward and tried to lift the body of the Scotsman. It was stuck fast to the ground. It was only then that the men realized that the pitchfork had been driven through the tail of McIntyre's raincoat by some supernatural force, pinning the disbelieving Scotsman to the ground.

McIntyre had seen the ghost of the drowned man and had died of fright.

13

The Ghost in the Alley

ST. JOHN'S, NEWFOUNDLAND

Rumors were rife about the alleyway behind the tavern. It was haunted, folks said. Haunted by the ghost of a young girl who had been found murdered in that self-same passage. People avoided the small street after dark, for the spirit was said to be a vengeful one, and—according to the stories—she had taken more than one life in her quest to avenge her death. Of course, no one could name who had been killed by the ghost. It was always "someone from out of town." But the tales were enough to keep people away from the alley at night, though it was frequently used as a shortcut to the main road during the day.

Fortunately for the owners of the tavern that backed onto the alley, their front door faced a well-lit road and so business was not slack, even with a reputed ghost in their back pocket. In fact, people sometimes came to drink there and discuss the story of the vengeful ghost in the alleyway behind.

Then one night, while the tavern was full of drinkers, a nasty character named O'Hare wandered into the bar. The bartender looked upon him with distaste, for his reputation was a foul one. Women and children were not safe in his presence.

Mothers whisked their young daughters away from his vicinity if he so much as looked at them, and the children in town were carefully instructed to avoid him. O'Hare had also been known to pick a fight with the men in town over the least little incident. But he paid cash for all his drinks, and so the bartender was instructed to serve him, though he never lingered to chat.

When O'Hare had consumed far too much alcohol, he suddenly announced to the bar that he'd seen a pretty young thing in the alley out back of the tavern. The bartender froze in the middle of polishing a glass, and the men around the bar exchanged covert glances. No one said a word, but everyone was thinking about the ghost of the vengeful young girl. The bartender could not imagine who else would be hanging about the alley at this time of night, since everyone in town avoided walking there after dark.

"I'm going to go talk to her," O'Hare stuttered drunkenly with a leer. Everyone in the bar looked down at their glasses as he stumbled to his feet. No one made a move to stop him, and no one mentioned the ghost. There was a quiet air of "he deserves what's coming to him" about the bar as O'Hare left the building.

"I hope the ghost gets him," someone muttered into his ale. No one bothered looking to see who had voiced the sentiment, since it was one they all shared. *It's just too bad that there isn't really a ghost,* thought the bartender, setting down the shining glass and picking up another one to polish. O'Hare sorely needed a lesson in human kindness and respect for others.

At that moment, a horrible scream came from the alley. Everyone in the tavern looked up in shock and fear. Had there

THE GHOST IN THE ALLEY

really been a ghost out there? Or was O'Hare up to his old tricks and even now accosting one of their womenfolk?

The men leapt to their feet and raced as one to the back door of the tavern. Pouring out into the street, they were met by an unnatural cold, and their eyes dazzled by a blaze of light.

The bartender thrust his way to the front of the crowd and saw the body of O'Hare lying in a pool of bright white light. His throat had been torn to pieces, and blood was spilling out in gushes. Above him hovered the semitransparent figure of a young girl, her eyes gleaming with red fire, her mouth covered with blood. She glared down at O'Hare and then turned to look at the crowd. All the men took a giant step backward, their eyes fixed on the ghost. The specter licked the blood from her lips thoughtfully, her eyes on the bartender's neck. Then she vanished, taking the light with her, and at their feet, O'Hare gasped out his last breath and died.

With a shout of terror, the men beat a hasty retreat back into the bar. The local authorities were summoned to deal with the body of O'Hare. Though skeptical at first, they were finally convinced of the facts surrounding the evil man's death, since there had been so many eyewitnesses who had seen the ghost in the alley hovering over the dying man.

The bartender resigned his position the next morning and took a job across town, the memory of the ghost's hungry stare at his neck prompting him to look elsewhere for employment. No one blamed him one bit, and after that day the alley was shunned by all. Nobody wanted to chance meeting the ghost again.

14

I'm Coming Down Now!

Well, now, there was an abandoned house sitting in the middle of a fancy neighborhood in Calgary that nobody would go near on a dare. And I mean nobody. Not even those crazy schoolkids! They were too frightened of the ghost that haunted the place to set foot in the yard, and folks refused to walk down the road at night for fear of what they might hear and see.

The neighbors were always complaining to the authorities about the moaning and screaming and maniacal laughter that came from the house every night. A few cautious visits to the place were made by the police, but each ended the same way: with the officer getting chased out of the house by the haunt (and pelted with old boots all the way down the street). Finally, the local authorities refused to send anyone back to the house again, and the neighbors were told to either live with the ghost or move.

Now, my pal Albert was the agent in charge of selling that haunted house, and he'd tried everything in his power to close a deal. He'd had a priest in to bless the place (in two minutes flat the priest jumped out a window and went running for his life). He'd had a couple of mediums in to converse with the spirits (last I heard, both those ladies were doing quite nicely in the local insane asylum—as long as folks were careful not to mention ghosts in their hearing). He'd even contacted a hoodoo doctor from down in the States to do some spells on the house, but the fellow turned tail as soon as he set foot on the road in front of the house, leaving behind a scattering of hoodoo dolls stuck with needles, goofer dust, and strange-looking potions in glass bottles.

Finally, Albert lit on the notion of selling the house sight unseen to a rich city slicker from the States who wanted a place in the "wilds" of Canada. Worked like a charm, too. The fellow was eager to sign the papers, and Albert thought he'd finally got the place off his hands. Until the city slicker decided he wanted to visit the property after all. Albert was all set to take the fellow there at high noon when presumably the ghost was asleep, but the city slicker's train was delayed, so it wasn't until after dinner that the two men set off for the haunted house. It was a dark and rainy night, but early enough in the evening that the ghost might still be resting wherever it was that ghosts went to sleep. At least, Albert hoped this was the case.

The house looked quiet and peaceful in the misty darkness as the two men stepped through the wrought-iron gate and onto the overgrown pathway toward the sagging front porch.

"Needs a little work," Albert said. "But that's why you're getting such a good bargain."

"Just what I'd expect from the wild west!" the city slicker drawled happily. "You know, this place looks like it could be haunted!"

Albert started violently. "Nope! No ghosts here!" he stuttered, crossing his fingers hopefully.

He unlocked the front door, and it opened with an ominous creak that boded no good for those who dared enter. Albert swallowed nervously, but the city slicker just chuckled and said something about atmosphere. Albert relaxed a bit. This fellow was just too naïve to be true, he thought, and wondered if he shouldn't have raised the price a bit.

The two men entered a tall foyer absolutely festooned with dusty cobwebs.

"Creepy!" the city slicker said enthusiastically. He bounded energetically into the center of the foyer, faced the sweeping staircase to the upper story and raised his arms dramatically. "Come to me, foul spirits!" he intoned loudly.

Albert gasped in dismay. Was this fellow plumb loco?

The city slicker whirled away from the grand staircase and was peering into the front parlor when the whole house rang with a sinister, unearthly chuckle. The laughter grew louder, taking on a maniacal edge that made Albert's hair stand on end. And then the voice spoke: "I'm coming down now!" it boomed. The phantom overtones in the deep voice reached right down Albert's spine and tautened every nerve in his body.

The city slicker jumped and then turned to Albert with a happy grin. "Great special effects! How'd you do that?"

"I didn't," Albert said, his teeth chattering. He backed up until he hit the front door and stood there with his hand on the knob, staring up the grand staircase in fear.

"I'm coming down now!" the voice boomed again, and

the city slicker's grin slipped a bit. He looked at Albert's frightened posture and then followed the agent's gaze toward the stairs.

A bright light exploded into being at the top of the steps and quickly resolved into a sinister green head with flaming eyes, writhing hair, and fangs instead of teeth. The head opened its mouth and screamed; a terrible, high-pitched sound that scraped across the nerves and set the legs running before the brain had a chance to kick in.

As the head began rolling down the stairs toward the two men, Albert's nerve broke. He scrabbled at the door handle for a moment, realized he had to turn the knob to the right instead of the left, and a moment later was halfway down the road, his own scream rivaling that of the specter in the house behind him.

It wasn't until he was almost home that he realized that he had company. The city slicker was running along beside him and was setting a pretty fast pace.

"Mister, I don't think I want that house after all," he panted when he saw Albert's gaze upon him.

"Why not?" asked a hauntingly familiar voice from the far side of the city slicker. Albert and the city slicker looked over and saw the green head with flaming red eyes keeping pace with them as they raced down the street.

The city slicker gave a screech that would have shamed a banshee, leapt five feet straight up into the air, and disappeared into the distance so fast there was no keeping up with him.

"Must have been the asking price," the floating head said conversationally to Albert. The real estate agent shrieked even

I'M COMING DOWN NOW!

louder than the city slicker and ran away so fast that his shoes made sparks against the pavement.

"Was it something I said?" the green head called after Albert, but the agent was already around the bend and out of sight. With a wicked chuckle, the phantom head disappeared in a puff of sulfurous smoke.

The next day, Albert quit his job and moved to Vancouver, where he spent the rest of his life working on a fishing boat. The owner of the haunted house finally sold the property to the city, and the authorities sent a wrecking crew out on a bright summer day at noon to tear it down. There's a shoe store there now, and so far no one's reported any ghostly heads hovering over the merchandise. But I sure wouldn't buy shoes there, nohow!

The Wallflower

She stood at the fringes of the crowded dance floor, watching wistfully as the other girls danced and flirted with the boys. He in turn watched her. He'd never seen her before, but that did not concern him. Often the girls brought visiting friends and relations to the local dances. Or perhaps he had just missed seeing her before in the frequently crowded dance hall.

She was beautiful, with a willowy figure, sparkling green eyes, and curly black hair. She was the sort of girl he usually avoided, since he was short, plain, and too outspoken by half. The fact that he was probably the most intelligent and well-read boy in the room, with a keen sense of humor that made his friends and family laugh until they had to beg him to stop telling jokes, didn't seem to matter much to the frivolous set of girls in his school and church. At least, not yet. (In later years, he would become the most pursued bachelor in Winnipeg. But that was in the future.)

He had no partner that night at the dance. His invitation had been turned down by two girls, one at school and one at church, each of whom preferred to go out with one of the popular boys on the hockey team. After those experiences, he hesitated to approach the green-eyed girl, but she looked so lonely and wistful that he slowly made his way toward her, skirting the dancers, until he stood at her side.

"It's a beautiful night," he ventured during a break in the music. The girl turned toward him in surprise, and he got a good look at her. She was wearing a long white dress, slightly out of date, with delicate pink roses embroidered along the tight sleeves and hem.

After studying him a moment uncertainly, she smiled and agreed with him. He asked her name, and was told she was called Sarah after her grandmother. He responded with his own name, and they fell into easy conversation. Finally, he asked her to dance, but she blushed shyly and told him she could not. She whisked her skirts to one side for a moment, lest he be offended by her refusal, and he saw a brace around her leg and ankle. Now it was his turn to flush in embarrassment.

To make up for his blunder, he found her a chair in a secluded corner that offered a good view of the dance floor and brought her some punch to drink. Together, they sat out all the songs, laughing and talking as if they'd known one another all their lives rather than having met for the first time that evening.

He hesitated shyly before volunteering to drive her home in his brand-new Ford Touring Car. She blushed daintily and then accepted. The early autumn night had grown cold, and when he asked about her wrap, she told him that she did not have one. Immediately he whipped off his jacket and tucked it around her thin shoulders before helping her into the front seat of his car.

They drove toward her home in silence, Sarah humming happily to herself. And then, between one note and the next, Sarah vanished from the seat beside him. He gasped and hit the brake. *What? How?* He searched his car, then he searched the street, his car blocking the roadway until an impatient traveler honked the horn and he moved it.

Sarah was gone and he didn't have a clue how she had disappeared so quickly. He hadn't even seen her open the door! And he'd been driving at quite a clip. If she'd jumped out, there should have been some sign of a fall or at least some heavy running footprints in the dirt road as she tried to maintain her balance against the speed. But why should she run away? They were having such a good time, and he was being a perfect gentleman.

Then he pictured again the way she had seemed to simply vanish into thin air, and the hairs on his arms stood on end while a shudder went through him. It seemed almost supernatural. Finally, upset and concerned, he made his way to the address she had given him, which stood next to an old church cemetery, and knocked on the door, hoping that Sarah had somehow already made it home.

He heard voices coming from the front parlor, where a light still shone. He shivered in the cold as he waited, for Sarah had been wearing his jacket when she disappeared. Then a pretty, middle-aged lady who looked like an older version of Sarah opened the door. Stumbling a little, he explained that he had met Sarah at the dance, but that she had disappeared while he was escorting her home, and he was concerned for her safety. At his words, the lady turned pale, grabbed the door pane with trembling hands, and called for her husband to come at once.

Her husband, a burly no-nonsense authority figure, hurried to the door, and his wife made the boy repeat his tale. She even made him describe Sarah's dress in detail, and he mentioned that they'd sat out all the songs because of her injured leg. By the time he finished, the tall man looked as shaken as his wife. He brushed a hand across his face to hide some strong emotion, and then said: "Son, today is the one-year anniversary of our daughter Sarah's death. She was killed in a car accident on her way home from a dance. Her escort got drunk and crashed the car into a ditch at exactly the place you say she disappeared."

The boy whitened. "That's impossible!" he gasped.

Sarah's mother smiled weakly, went inside for a moment, and came out carrying a framed picture. The green-eyed, black-curled girl in the photo was wearing a white dress embroidered with pink roses on the sleeves and hem. "This picture was taken the night she died," the mother said. "Sarah sewed the dress herself to wear to the dance."

Seeing him struggling with disbelief, the husband grabbed a coat from the hall closet, offered another to the shivering lad—which he gratefully accepted—and led the way to the church cemetery next door to their house, where Sarah lay buried. As they walked through the gleaming moonlight, he spoke sadly but fondly of his beautiful daughter, who had loved to dance and sing and was planning on attending college

THE WALLFLOWER

when she finished high school. The boy listened soberly, his logical mind still struggling to accept the facts that the parents had presented him.

Then his eye was caught by a graceful tombstone directly ahead, which was draped with something that appeared dark and shapeless in the moonlight. He gasped and ran forward, then fell to his knees in front of the grave. He felt the father's hand drop sympathetically on his shoulder as his fingers clutched the sleeve of his own jacket, so recently gracing Sarah's shoulders, and now wreathing her tomb. His eyes were glued to the words carved near the top of the stone, which he read over and over again, trying to take them in. The words said simply: "In loving memory of Sarah."

PART TWO
Powers of Darkness and Light

16

The Flying Canoe

GATINEAU, QUEBEC

Ah, that Baptiste! He was a naughty one, *mon fils,* yes, indeed. Tall as a mountain, strong as an ox, with muscles that rippled along the whole length of him; that was Baptiste. A handsome face, with dark flashing eyes and a rippling black beard; that was Baptiste. A lover of drinking, dancing, and flirting; *oui,* that was also Baptiste. He was a heartbreaker with *les dames.*

He was a mighty lumberjack who faced the very broadest and tallest trees without fear, though a tree is a tricksome thing that would as soon crush a lumberjack as fall straight and true to the ground. Baptiste had a double-edged axe that was so long and so broad that no one save himself could lift it. When he came forth from the lumber camp each spring, he was hailed with gasps of joy from the women and envious muttering from the men, who lost all their girls to Baptiste the minute he showed his face in town.

Baptiste was a shining star among the lumberjacks, who went to work each winter in the center of a very large forest, chopping down mammoth trees and watching them crash into the thick snow in exactly the place where they said the trees would land. Then they would cut up the trees and haul them hither and thither. They worked hard, *mon Dieu*, very hard indeed! But it was a lonely life for them, with wives and sweethearts left behind. And even the tales and exploits of Baptiste could not keep them from longing for home.

On New Year's Day, it snowed so hard that no work could be done. The men huddled in their camp and spoke longingly of their loved ones back in town. They passed around the rum and drank toasts to the New Year, but finally Baptiste said what they were all thinking: "I wish to go home today and see my girl!"

There were murmurs of agreement from all. With a lonely sign, Jean-Claude replied: "How can we go home today? There is more than two meters of snow on the road, and more snow is falling."

"Ah, *mon ami!* Who said we were walking out of here?" asked Baptiste. "I am going to paddle out in my canoe." The men went still and stared at Baptiste, their eyes wide.

The lumberjacks had all heard the story, of course. A dark man with a sharp face, glowing red eyes, and hooves where his feet should have been had been seen talking with Baptiste out back of the lumber camp shortly after the first snowfall. The lumberjack who had witnessed the conversation swore it was the Devil. According to the eavesdropper, Baptiste had promised the Devil that he would not say the Mass for an entire year if the Evil One would allow him to visit his sweetheart in town whenever he wished during the long winter months when he was tied to the lumber camp. And the Devil had agreed.

Shortly after this conversation, a large black canoe had appeared in the woods behind the camp. The canoe was decorated from top to bottom with archaic symbols in a red dye that looked as if it might be human blood. On dark nights, the symbols glowed, casting evil red shadows among the trees. And strangest of all, the canoe seemed to whisper to itself in a strange tongue that sounded like the hiss of snakes. No one save Baptiste would go near the wicked thing.

"*La chasse gallerie,*" Jean-Claude whispered at last, his eyes so wide that the whites showed. "The flying canoe."

Baptiste smiled the devil-may-care grin that made all the ladies swoon.

"I may fly where I wish," Baptiste said grandly. "To town to see my sweetheart or to the ends of the earth, it matters not."

"There must be a catch, *mon ami,*" Jean-Claude protested. "There is always a catch somewhere."

"Just two conditions," said Baptiste carelessly. "No Mass for a year."

"And the other?" asked Jean-Claude suspiciously. The other lumberjacks strained forward, agog to hear what Baptiste would say.

"Everyone who rides with me in the canoe must be home before dawn or their souls are forfeit," said Baptiste calmly. "Oh, and we cannot say the name of God or fly over *une église* (a church) or touch a cross. If we do, the canoe will crash."

The lumberjacks sat back quickly at that. A forfeit soul or a terrible crash down from the sky seemed too high a risk to take, even for a night with their sweethearts. One by one, the men emptied their cups, rose, and left the fire, until only seven men remained sitting with Baptiste.

"Well, *mes amis*," said Baptiste softly, gazing from one rugged face to the next, "shall we go?"

Slowly, the seven men nodded and laid aside their mugs of rum. They followed Baptiste silently to the back of the lumber camp, tramping through the snow to the place where the canoe lurked, hissing to itself in the falling snow. The *chasse gallerie* began to glow as they approached it; the pulsing red symbols lighting up the snow and making it seem as if they were walking through great pools of blood.

Baptiste gestured for the men to get into the glowing canoe, and he handed out the paddles. Then he took his place at the front, raised his arms toward the tops of the trees and the cloudy, snow-filled sky, and chanted: "Acabris! Acabras! Acabram!" The words boomed through the woods, filled with a terrible power that bound Baptiste to the Devil even as it filled the evil canoe with life. The red symbols painted across the black hull flared so brightly that the men were forced to cover their eyes. Then the red light went out with a popping sound. In the sudden pitch dark, the canoe rose from the snowy ground.

Jean-Claude gave a soft gasp of fear and astonishment, and the other men murmured to themselves in amazement. At the front, Baptiste laughed in triumph. As they cleared the tree-tops, the snow ceased and the moon came out. Baptiste instructed the men to paddle toward town. Dipping the paddles into the crisp night air as if it were the waters of a river, the men turned the canoe to the east and set off for home.

There was a New Year's dance being held in the town hall, and the women almost swooned with delight when their menfolk made a grand entrance just after midnight. The lumberjacks were showered with kisses, and all the eligible females abandoned their escorts to surround Baptiste. He put his arm around his sweetheart, but kept a wicked eye on the other ladies as well, charming a kiss out of more than a few as he danced and drank and laughed his way through the night.

It was Jean-Claude who suddenly realized how close it was to dawn. With a gasp of horror, he abandoned his little wife and ran across the dance floor to Baptiste, who was seated on the floor with his back against the wall, legs half under a table, and a huge jug of rum at his side. Baptiste's sweetheart gave an annoyed screech as Jean-Claude pulled her off the big man's lap and tossed her aside as he attempted to shake Baptiste back to consciousness. They had to get home by dawn or forfeit their souls to the Devil.

The other lumberjacks, seeing Jean-Claude's panic, were shaken back to their senses. Calling out hasty farewells, they picked up Baptiste by his mighty arms and legs and staggered outside to where they had left the evil black canoe. It crouched still and silent behind a pile of brush, waiting and watching like a predator about to pounce. The men found its silence far more terrifying than its hissing and pulsing had been. It almost seemed that the canoe was disappointed that they had returned to it before dawn.

Still, the terror of losing their souls to the Devil was enough to drive the men onward. They flung themselves forward and threw Baptiste into the front of the canoe. Leaping in behind him, they called and shook him until he was awake enough to chant the magic words given him by the Devil.

Then they were aloft and paddling as fast as they could toward the camp, while Baptiste flopped over into the bottom of the canoe and started to snore.

It was Jean Claude who remembered the second clause in the Devil's contract. No one could say the name of God while they were in flight, or the canoe would crash. And Baptiste, in his drunken state, would almost certainly start swearing and taking the Lord's name in vain as soon as he awoke. Carefully, Jean Claude leaned forward from his seat, which was directly behind Baptiste, and tied his scarf over the lumberjack's mouth so that he would not be able to speak should he wake before they landed.

It was nearly dawn and they were almost home when Baptiste awoke, sat up, and started tugging on the gag in his mouth. He managed to loosen the scarf before Jean-Claude could reach him, and shouted: "*Mon Dieu,* why have you gagged me?"

As the name of God filled the air, all the red symbols painted on the sides of the canoe pulsed at once, a bright flare that blinded the men. They dropped their paddles and covered their eyes and ears as terrible, screeching voices began to howl from inside the wood of the canoe. One after another, ephemeral white forms burst from the sides of the vessel and flew away in fright. As each departed, the black canoe lurched in the night sky, and when the last evil spirit had fled before the name of God, the canoe plunged rapidly toward the ground.

The men screamed, clutching the sides of the craft as if this would help break their fall. Then the canoe smashed into the top of a large pine tree, and all the men tumbled out and fell,

THE FLYING CANOE

down toward a gaping dark hole that snapped open in the earth beneath them. It looked like the open jaws of a shark, waiting to swallow them whole. In its depths, the lumberjacks could see the raging red fires of hell.

Baptiste and the other men plunged into the hole, and it snapped shut behind them with a sharp cracking sound that echoed throughout the forest. In the treetop, the broken black canoe pulsed again with a blinding red light, and then disappeared in a puff of sulfurous smoke.

Baptiste and his seven companions were never seen again.

17

Maid of the Mist

NIAGARA FALLS, ONTARIO

I do not consider myself a coward. I have always faced whatever dangers life threw at me with a brave heart and steady hands. But now my hands were shaking as they gripped the paddle. My canoe was caught in the current and there was no turning back, even had I wished it. And I did not wish it, for life was very bitter to me, and I desired a swift end to my anguish. I had buried my husband before his time, and all that was left within me was a terrible pain that could not be healed. After many days of mourning, I realized I could not go on, and I had decided that death would be better than agony.

But when I heard the distant roaring of the great falls, my hands had begun trembling, and the peace I had felt when I first set foot in my canoe fled. It was, I think, the realization that there would be physical pain before death that made me shiver and shake. I prayed to the Thunderer that my death would be swift and that my courage would remain with me until the end.

I threw my useless paddle away as the canoe entered the rapids and I watched the falls growing nearer, the sky reaching down to touch the very edge of the water as it plunged into the abyss. I gripped the sides of the canoe as the current heaved the small craft to and fro, moving me swiftly to my end. I sang softly to myself, a death song that I had been composing for many days. There was no one to hear me, even if I could sing loudly enough to pierce through the thunder of the falls, but that was no matter.

The turmoil of the water under my canoe increased, but it did not hide the thunder of the cataract. I could feel droplets and soon enough I would see the clouds of mist boiling upward from the abyss. Those clouds would screen my final seconds, and for that I was thankful.

My canoe reached the brink and seemed to hang for an eternal moment at the edge of the chasm. I leapt to my feet with a cry, determined to show bravery at the end in spite of my trembling. And then I was falling, falling through the clouds of mist.

I had expected pain and swift death. Instead, I was caught and held in a strong pair of arms. I looked up through the swirling mist into the face of my rescuer. In his face I saw the wisdom of the ancients, and his eyes, though fierce, were kind. He did not speak, but his voice was all around me, in the roar of the cataract above which we were floating. He was Heno, the Thunderer. He had heard my prayer, and instead of giving me the courage to die, was giving me a second chance to live.

We floated to the great curtain of water, and he shielded me with his body as he stepped through it into the cavern behind the falls. He placed me on a stone bench in the dim twilight behind the falls, and for the first time since I had buried my husband, I broke down and wept out my anguish at his passing and my relief at my rescue.

Heno spoke to me then, and his voice was kind. He told me I could live here with him and his family as long as I wished, until my pain had healed. I thanked him, and he showed me to a room where I could change into dry clothing and rest.

I met his sons when I awoke from the first healing sleep I had had since my husband's death. Even through the anguish I felt at my loss, my heart recognized that the Thunderer's younger son mattered to me in a way that no one else—not even my late husband—had ever mattered. I did not speak of my feelings to him at that time, or in the slow, healing days and weeks that followed. But somehow, he sensed when my heart was ready, and he came to me at that time with soft words of friendship, which swiftly grew into the flames of love.

Heno was pleased by the match, and even better pleased with our son, whom he trained in the ways of the Thunderer. I was as happy now as I had once been sad, and the only thing I missed from my old life was knowledge of my people. Heno sensed my longing, and he would sometimes check on my village and tell me all he had heard and seen of them. And so many seasons passed in peace and prosperity.

Then one day, Heno appeared in the cavern where I was working. I saw at once that the Thunderer, my husband's father, was troubled. When I asked him what was wrong, the Thunderer told me that a great snake had poisoned the waters of my people and that it would soon return to devour the dead until my people were all gone. I was horrified and asked him

MAID OF THE MIST

what I could do to avert this tragedy. Heno told me that I should go back—just for an hour—and warn my people of the danger. I consented at once, and the Thunderer lifted me through the mighty curtain of water and up, over the falls to the gathering place in my village.

For a few moments, I stood once more among my people, eagerly seeking out familiar faces as I gave them warning about the evil snake that was causing such pestilence among them. I advised them to move to a higher country until the danger had passed, and they agreed. Then Heno came and lifted me up into his arms and took me home.

It was but a few days later that the giant serpent returned to my village, seeking the bodies of those who had died from the poison it had spread. When the snake realized that the people had deserted the village, it hissed in rage and turned upstream, intent on pursuit.

But Heno had heard the voice of the serpent. He rose up through the mist of the falls and threw a great thunderbolt at the creature, killing it in one mighty blast. The giant body of the creature floated downstream and lodged just above the cataract, creating a large semicircle that deflected huge amounts of water into the falls at the place just above our home. Horrified by this disastrous turn of events, Heno swept in through the falls and did his best to stop the massive influx of water, but it was too late.

Seeing that our home would soon be destroyed, the Thunderer called for me and his sons to come away with him. My husband caught me and our child up in his embrace, and followed Heno through the water of the falls and up into the sky, where the Thunderer made us a new home. From this place, we watch over the people of the earth, while Heno thunders in the clouds as he once thundered in the vapors of the great falls. And still to this day, an echo of the Thunderer's voice can be heard at Niagara Falls.

18

Attack of the Mammoth

FORT WARE, BRITISH COLUMBIA

The man and his family were constantly moving, hunting for beaver. They traveled from lake to lake, stream to stream, never staying any place long enough for it to become a home. The woman sometimes silently wished that they would find a village and settle down somewhere with their little baby. But her husband was restless, and so they kept moving.

One evening, after setting up camp on a large lake, the young mother went out to net some beaver, carrying her baby upon her back. When she had a toboggan full of beaver meat, she started back to camp. As she walked through the darkening evening, she heard the thump-thump-thump of mighty footsteps coming from somewhere behind her. She stopped, her heart pounding. She was being followed by something very large. Her hands trembled as she thought of the meat she was dragging behind her. The creature must have smelled the meat and was stalking it.

Afraid to turn around and alert the beast, she bent over as if to pick something up off the snowy path and glanced quickly past her legs. Striding boldly through the snowy landscape was a tall, barrel-shaped, long-haired creature with huge tusks and a very long trunk. It was a tix—a mammoth—and it looked angry to see her in its territory. She straightened quickly and hurriedly threw the meat into the snow, hoping to appease the monster, which she had heard of but never seen until this moment. Then she ran as fast as she could back to camp, dragging the toboggan behind her. Her little baby cried out fearfully, frightened by all the jostling, but she did not stop to comfort him until she was safe inside their shelter.

She told her husband at once about the terrible mammoth that had stalked her. Her husband shook his head and told her she was dreaming. Everyone knew that the mammoth had all died away. Then he light-heartedly accused her of giving the meat away to a handsome sweetheart. She denied it resentfully, knowing that he really believed that she had carelessly overturned the toboggan and let the meat sink beneath the icy waters of the lake.

After her husband went to set more beaver nets, she prepared the evening meal. While it was cooking over the fire, she walked all around the camp, making sure that there was an escape route through the willow-brush just in case the terrible mammoth attacked them in the night.

The husband and wife lay down to sleep next to the fire after they finished the evening meal. The husband chuckled when he saw that his wife kept her moccasins on and the baby clutched in her arms. "Expecting the mammoth to attack us?" he asked jovially. She nodded, and he laughed aloud. Soon he was asleep, but the woman lay awake for a long time, listening.

The wife was awakened from a light doze around midnight

by the harsh sounds of the mammoth approaching. "Husband," she shouted, shaking him. He opened his eyes grumpily and demanded an explanation. She tried to tell him that an angry mammoth was stalking them, but he told her she was having a nightmare and would not listen.

The wife begged and pleaded and tried to drag him away with her, but he resisted and finally shouted at her to begone if she was afraid. In despair, she clutched her little child to her chest and ran away from the camp.

As she fled, she heard the harsh roar of the giant creature and the sudden shout of her husband as he came face to face with the creature. Then there was silence, and the woman knew her husband was dead. Weeping, she fled with her child, seeking a village that she had heard was nearby. Sometime in the early hours of the morning, she heard the thump-thump-thump of the creature's massive feet stomping through the snow fields, following her trail. Occasionally, it made a wailing sound like that of a baby crying.

The woman kept jogging along, comforting her little boy as best she could. As light dawned, she saw a camp full of people who were living on the shores of an island on the lake. She crossed the icy expanse as quickly as possible and warned the people of the fierce mammoth that had killed her husband. The warriors quickly went out onto the ice and made many holes around the edges of their village, weakening the ice so that the mammoth would fall through and drown if it approached.

As evening approached, the people saw the mammoth coming toward them across the ice. When it neared their camp

ATTACK OF THE MAMMOTH

on the island, the creature plunged through the weakened ice. Everyone cried out with joy, thinking that the animal would drown. But to their horror, they saw the beast raise its large, hairy head from the water, shake its long tusks, and bellow in rage. Then the mammoth started walking along the bottom of the lake, brushing aside the ice with his large tusks.

The people panicked. They screamed and ran in circles, and some of them stood frozen in place, staring as the mammoth emerged from the ice and walked up onto the banks of the island. The young wife fled with her baby, urging as many of her new-found friends as she could reach to flee with her. But many remained behind, paralyzed with fear.

Then a boy emerged from one of the shelters, curious to know what was causing everyone to scream in fear. He wore the bladder of a moose over his head, covering his hair so that he looked bald. He was a strange lad and was shunned by his people. Only his grandmother knew that he was a mighty shaman with magic trousers and magic arrows that could kill any living beast.

When the boy saw the angry mammoth, he called to his grandmother to fetch the magic trousers and the magic arrows. Donning his clothing, he shook his head until the bladder burst and his long hair fell down to his waist. Then he took his magic bow and arrows, leapt in front of the frightened people, and began peppering the beast with arrows, first from one side and then the other. The mammoth roared and weaved and tried to attack the boy, but the shaman's magic was powerful, and soon the beast lay dead upon the ground.

Then those who fled from the mammoth returned to the

camp, led by the poor widow and her baby. The people whose lives had been saved by the bladder-headed boy gave a cheer and gathered in excitement around him. In gratitude, they made the young shaman their chief and offered him two beautiful girls to be his wives, though he accepted only one of them. The widow and her baby were welcomed into the tribe, and a few months later she married a brave warrior who became close friends with the shaman-chief.

And from that day to this, the people have always had chiefs to lead them, and no mammoths have troubled them again.

19

The Devil and the Loup Garou

MONTREAL, QUEBEC

Now there once was a man named Jean Dubroise who never did a lick of work, but his house and his barn and his crops were still the best in the whole land. This puzzled all of the people in the vicinity, since Jean had no family and no hired men to help him. No one could figure out how he managed to have the best trapping lines in winter, and have fences and barns in perfect repair at all times with no one else working on his farm.

Stranger still were the reports of a roaring sound that came from Jean Dubroise's property late at night when all good, God-fearing people should be sleeping. It would start with a low rumble that shook the ground and caused the hairs to stand up at the back of the neck. Then the sound would grow and grow until the ears would pound and the body would jerk convulsively as if trying to rid itself of the noise.

Nothing reduced the intensity of the sound—not hands clamped over the ears or ear plugs or cotton stuffed into the ear channels. It pierced the skull and pounded through the bloodstream, and anyone who heard it was forced to lie down for an entire twenty-four hours to recover their wits and their strength. The neighbors on both sides of Dubroise's house sold out pretty quickly after the noise began, and people started avoiding the place. Townsfolk would hurry to the other side of the road rather than meet Jean when they saw him coming.

One night shortly after taking possession of his brand new property, Dubroise's newest next-door neighbor, Alphonse, stayed a bit too late in town, drinking with friends. On a dare, the drunken Alphonse decided that he would take a shortcut across Dubroise's land to get home.

As he was weaving his way through the fields, the ground under Alphonse's feet began to shake. Every hair on his head stood on end as a strange sound thrummed through the air and grew in intensity. Alphonse clapped his hands over his ears, which were ringing painfully, and his body started jerking convulsively as the terrible skull-piercing noise grew louder. Alphonse threw himself flat on the ground in agony. As he squirmed in the dirt, trying to find relief from the noise, he saw a huge canoe pop into existence out of nowhere with a final ear-splitting bang and fly out over the field.

As soon as the flying canoe appeared, the terrible noise heralding its approach ceased as abruptly as it had started. The canoe landed on the ground in the clearing next to the Dubroise house, and a tall man dressed all in black with wicked dark eyes, a short sharp beard, cloven hooves instead of feet, and two short horns on his head emerged from the canoe with a whip in his hand. It was the Devil!

THE DEVIL AND THE LOUP GAROU

At the sight of the Devil, Alphonse gasped and rolled under some shrubs at the edge of the field. From his hiding place, he heard the Devil shout: "Come out of the canoe!" He snapped his whip at the occupants. Twenty creatures with the shaggy coats of wolves but the upright walk of men leapt forward. Alphonse recognized them immediately. They were loup garou—men who had neglected their religious duties for so long that they had fallen under the spell of the Devil.

While the loup garou began plowing and mending fences and doing all the daily chores on the farm, Dubroise came out of his front door to talk and drink with the Devil. Alphonse knew then that Dubroise had sold his lazy soul to the Devil in exchange for the werewolves' work on his farm. Alphonse lay trembling under the bushes, praying the Devil and his minions wouldn't find him. After several hours of strenuous labor, the Devil and the loup garou jumped back into the enchanted canoe and flew away.

As soon as it was safe, Alphonse hurried to the local priest to report what he had seen. When he heard about Dubroise's evil visitors, the priest came up with a plan to rid the neighborhood of the Devil.

While Dubroise was in town the next day, the priest sent Alphonse and several of the parish men to Dubroise's farm with buckets full of holy water. The men sprinkled the holy water over Dubroise's house, his outbuildings, and all of his land. Then the men hid themselves in the thicket to keep watch.

It was midnight when the terrible noise heralding the approach of the flying canoe filled the pastures and woods of the Dubroise farm. All the men had stuffed their ears full of cloth blessed with holy water, which kept out the worst of the noise, and so they were not overcome when the Devil and the loup garou came flying down.

The canoe landed in the clearing next to the house, and the Devil leapt out immediately. As soon as his foot touched the holy water sprinkled onto the ground, he started leaping about and shrieking in pain and rage. Behind him, the werewolves were frightened and huddled inside the canoe, unsure what to do.

The Devil was furious. He believed that Dubroise was trying to save his soul by driving him away with holy water obtained from the priest. Cursing and blaspheming in a most foul manner, the Devil ran into the house and pulled Dubroise right out of his bed.

The loup garou were frightened by the Devil's anger, and slithered out of the canoe while he was inside the house, determined to put as much distance as possible between themselves and their terrible master. By the time the Devil dragged Jean Dubroise outside, the canoe was empty. The Devil threw Jean into the canoe and flew away in a blast of fire that scorched the ground for many meters.

When they were sure that the Devil was gone, the men of the parish came out from their hiding places, collected the frightened werewolves, and brought them to the priest. Knowing that a drop of blood would restore their true form, the priest pricked each loup garou on the finger with a knife blessed with holy water. One by one, as the drops of blood fell from their fingers, all of the loup garou turned back into men.

Immediately afterwards, the men fell to their knees and begged the priest to forgive them for neglecting their religious duties. From that day on, the men were faithful to their parish and never more did they fall under the Devil's spell. But Jean Dubroise was never seen again.

20

The Tolling of the Bell

CHARLOTTETOWN, PRINCE EDWARD ISLAND

I was new to the island back in October 1853, having just moved to Charlottetown from Nova Scotia. The wife and I both had kinfolk here; so it felt like coming home when we bought a little house in town and moved in.

We hadn't been here more than a few weeks when I was wakened one night by the tolling of a church bell late in the evening. I had Scottish blood in me and was always a little sensitive to the supernatural. When I heard the sound of the bell, I sat bolt upright, goose bumps all over my arms. My wife turned over to look at me. "Charlie, what's wrong?"

"That bell," I exclaimed, unable to express the feeling of dread the sound woke deep inside my shaking gut as I counted the bongs—one, two, three, four.

"Probably just a midnight service somewhere," my wife said.

"We'd have heard if there was a midnight service," I said, but at her insistence I lay back down, though I was sure that something was wrong. Then I sat up again in alarm. "Maybe it's a fire bell. I should go look!"

"It's not a fire bell. Go back to sleep," said my wife over the final two bongs—numbers seven and eight by my count. The bell stopped tolling then, and I settled back under the covers, trying to ignore the knot in my stomach and go back to sleep. I tried to tell myself it was nothing—that a goose had just walked over my grave. But somehow I was sure that the late-night bell was significant—both to me and to the town.

The story was all over Charlottetown the next morning. When I went into the dry goods store to make a purchase, one of the men who lived in a house near St. John's Church was talking excitedly about the incident to a small group of residents, one of whom was my first cousin. Ted waved me over and asked the man to repeat his story for my benefit. He was eager to do so and told the following tale.

In the wee hours of the morning, when all the good residents of Charlottetown should have been sleeping in their beds, the man had heard the deep, melancholy call of a bell from the tower in St. James Church. The somber sound rang out over the rooftops, waking him from a deep sleep with the unexpectedness of its doom-laden ring. Then a second toll rang slowly overhead, followed by a third.

Bewildered by the unexpected tolling of the bell and suspecting mischief from some of the more disreputable boys in town, the man had raced outside in his nightshirt, intent on investigating. He was met by his next-door neighbor, and the two men hurriedly joined forces in the road outside their homes and went to investigate. Above them, the bell tolled for the fourth time, and then again for the fifth time.

As they entered the churchyard, the bell tolled for the sixth time, and the front doors of the church swung open with a windy blast. Framed in the doorway were three glowing women dressed all in white. The men gasped, unsure if they were seeing real women or angels. Overhead, the bell tolled for a seventh time, and the doors slammed shut as quickly as they had opened. The men raced to the doors and tugged on the handles, but they were firmly locked. When they peered through the windows, the men saw one of the glowing women ascending the stairs to the belfry.

The minister and the sexton arrived at that moment, demanding to know what the disturbance was about. The neighbors told the new arrivals what they had seen, and the minister unlocked the door to the church. As they entered the vestibule, they saw no sign of the women the neighbors had seen in the doorway. A quick glance through the church revealed not a living soul.

As the men ascended the belfry, the bell tolled for the eighth time. They ran up the last few steps, determined to confront the women in white and demand an explanation. When they reached the top, they found the belfry empty and the bell rope tied firmly in place, though the metal of the church bell was still vibrating slightly.

The men stood staring at the shaking bell in shock. The staircase was the only way in or out of the belfry. Unless the women had flung themselves out the window? The sexton rushed to look, but to his relief he saw no bodies lying helpless and broken on the ground below.

Puzzled and frightened, the minister and his companions

THE TOLLING OF THE BELL

searched the church from top to bottom, but it was completely empty. As the bell gave no further sign of tolling, the men left the church, mystified by what had happened.

When the man finished his tale, everyone in the shop agreed that it was a peculiar circumstance, and wondered together what it might portend. A terrible storm, a plague, and a death at sea were just a few of the wild ideas bandied about. A few of the less superstitious among us thought it must have been kids playing a prank on the minister and sexton, and that the men had just missed their hiding place in the heat of the moment.

I went home and reported the news to the wife. She was busy cleaning up the spare bedroom, since we were expecting one of her innumerable cousins to arrive that evening from Nova Scotia, and hardly paid attention to a word I said. I gave up finally and went out to harness the horse to our carriage for the drive down to the dock.

I waited for a long time in the October chill with several others who were expecting folks on the steamer. It never arrived. I turned back for home finally, when it was obvious that the boat would not come that night, with the same sick feeling in my stomach that I had felt when I heard the bell tolling in the night. Something was wrong. Something had happened to the steamer.

My wife thought it was a bit strange that the steamer hadn't arrived, but she failed to find it ominous. She was sure her cousin would show up the next day with some dramatic tale to tell about an engine failure or some other mechanical problem.

But the morning failed to bring the *Fairie Queen,* and news about the ship, when it finally came, was grim. The *Fairie Queen* had sunk en route to Prince Edward Island, killing the eight passengers who had boarded her that day—one of whom was my wife's cousin.

I remembered then that the men had seen three women in white inside the church as the bell sounded. And there were three women who had died on board the *Fairie Queen.* I shivered and pulled my weeping wife close to me, picturing in my mind the guardian spirits of five men and three women slowly ascending the bell tower and each ringing the bell once to signal the doom that awaited them the next morning. Fanciful of me, perhaps, but I've always been convinced that that was the true explanation for what happened on the night the bell tolled in Charlottetown.

21

The Lady with the O'er-Kind Eyes

GASPÉ PENINSULA, QUEBEC

The soft slap-slap of the water against the hull of the riverboat was the only sound in the misty twilight. Wisps of fog kept drifting across the wheelman's face, making him blink against the droplets of water that peppered his cheeks and eyes. He gripped the wheel a little tighter, cursing softly to himself. He hated the misty gloom that sometimes fell on the Saint Lawrence. It felt unnatural, somehow. A man could almost believe that strange, fey creatures lurked amidst the trees on shore, waiting for the cover of darkness to pounce upon the unwary.

The wheelman shivered and crossly told himself to stop thinking such nonsense. Nonetheless, he found his eyes straying quickly back and forth across the dark waters of the river, picturing twisted creatures in his mind. Then he shook his head sharply, for it was not some demon being that was slowly approaching him from the shoreline; rather, it was a light boat, rowed by the robed figure of a man. He was too indistinct to be seen clearly through the mist, and the stroke of his oars was absolutely noiseless. He was accompanied by a woman; a very beautiful woman indeed, the wheelman noted. Odd that he could see the woman so clearly, even through the mist, but not the man.

He dismissed the thought at once as a clear, alluring female voice hailed him from the boat. The sound of her voice roused the lethargic crew like a splash of cold water in the face, and to the wheelman's secret amusement, the captain came on deck at a run and ordered him to heave-to.

The wheelman stood at the rail, watching the exchange between the captain and the lady. She was plainly dressed, save for a blood-red scarf that exactly matched her ruby-red lips. The sight of that mouth made him shudder, and he found himself staring at her eyes, his heart pounding in fear. They were dark, fathomless eyes with a green, cat-like gleam that occasionally darted across the surface in a disconcerting manner. And even close up, he couldn't make out the face of the robed man. He felt a prickling sensation along his arms, and the hairs on the back of his neck stood on end. He peered closer at the man in the boat, and the figure wavered, as if it were somehow not fully present.

Beside him, the captain had finished passage negotiations with the woman, and she was brought aboard. As they got underway, the wheelman watched the rower surreptitiously as he returned to the far shore. Halfway there, boat and man winked out of existence. The wheelman gasped and suddenly found the dark-eyed, red-mouthed woman before him.

"And this is your faithful wheelman," she murmured softly

to the captain, her o'er kind eyes fixed upon his wind-roughed face and scraggly black beard. He straightened unconsciously under her seductive gaze, all thoughts of the rower driven out of his head. Her presence filled his mind like a sweet perfume, his body tingling to life at her gentle smile. She turned away then, and he sighed with regret and longing.

As the dusk darkened to night, he watched his captain strolling above deck with the lady. All the men were fixated on this woman with the o'er-kind eyes and the gracious manner. If she stopped to speak to one of the sailors, the seaman would blush red as a rose and stutter almost incoherently until she was gone. The foggy gloom of the river and the evil specters he had envisioned were forgotten in the wheelman's fascination with the lady.

He was unsure how much time passed—minutes, perhaps even hours—when his dazzled ears became aware of another sound that was gradually drowning out the dulcet murmurings of the lady as she spoke to the besotted captain. The wheelman's brow knit as he tried to recall where he'd heard that regular splashing ebb and flow sound before. Then, in a single instant, his cloudy brain cleared. Breakers! It was the crash of breakers against a reef. They had sailed unknowingly into the Gulf of Saint Lawrence.

He cried out to the sailors, to the captain, his eyes frantically piercing the gloom ahead of them. White water, directly ahead, and no time to turn.

At the rail, the lady with the o'er-kind eyes laughed, a shrill sound that cut through any remaining spell that lay over the minds of the crew. The wheelman tore his eyes from the

THE LADY WITH THE O'ER-KIND EYES

breakers to look at her. Her eyes were gleaming green like a cat's, and her blood-red lips were parted in a cruel smile that paralyzed his muscles. *Siren*, his mind screamed. She laughed at him and flung her body over the rail into the pounding waves.

Then the ship smashed into the reef, the hull splintering into pieces and water pouring in. The men were flung into the roiling sea as the ship foundered and sank. The wheelman could hear his shipmates screaming for help as their bodies were swept beneath the roaring waves. The wheelman grabbed a passing piece of driftwood and tried to get on top of it, hoping to float over the killer waves to safety. But he was pulled back into the water by a pair of entwining arms. Looking over his shoulder, he saw a pair of enticing green, o'er-kind eyes and a red mouth. The very last thing he heard was a triumphant laugh.

Tammatuyuq

HUDSON BAY, NUNAVUT

I walked swiftly through the aurora-lit *iglu* village, snuggling gratefully into the warmth of my caribou parka as I returned to my snow house after a busy afternoon out. My friend Nauja, my elder by a year, was to be married soon to a great hunter, and we were sewing her wedding clothes, making many beautiful patterns with beadwork to tell the world her status as a new wife.

On my left, I saw Amaruq passing by on his way to feed his sled dogs. He waved and I blushed, giggling a little and waving back. Sometime soon, Amaruq would ask for my hand in marriage. Then Nauja would come to my ice house and help *me* sew *my* wedding gown. But that day was not today.

I turned in at the door of the family ice house, passing with bowed head along the narrow, roofed passage of snow blocks until I arrived at the doorway (a hole at my feet), which I traversed on hands and knees until the main room opened out in front of me.

I rose and smiled at the bright light gleaming from the lamp—a saucer-shaped vessel of stone, filled with burning seal-oil—that hung two feet above the floor. A stone cooking pot was suspended above it, filling the snow house with a delicious smell.

Behind the lamp were some bags containing meat and blubber; in front of it, a table scattered with carving tools. My old grandfather bent intently over two small stone-carved figures in the lamplight. Behind him, a low sleeping platform covered with skins occupied fully half the floor space. Grandfather was the only one home, and he looked up with a smile when I entered. "Nayummi," he said my name tenderly. "You are back early."

"Nauja's husband-to-be came to see her, so I left them alone together," I explained, standing on tip-toe to look in the simmering pot. My stomach rumbled, and I patted it absently, knowing that our meal would shortly be ready.

"How very kind of you," Grandfather said with a sly grin, knowing that I'd left because I found their love-talk a bit embarrassing.

I sat at the table with him and regarding the stone he was carving. "What are you making?" I asked.

"This is Tammatuyuq and the woman," he told me. I frowned. I had never heard of Tammatuyuq. Mentally translating the name, I said: "'The one who makes mistakes?'"

"That is the literal translation," my grandfather said. "But do not be fooled by the name. It is an evil demon in the form of a woman, and it does terrible things."

I sensed a story. "Would you tell me about the Tammatuyuq, Grandfather?"

He glanced sharply at me. "It is not a nice story, little

mother," he said. (I am named after my great-grandmother.) "It may give you nightmares."

I lifted my head proudly. "I am nearly a woman grown," I told him. "Next year, Amaruq will ask for my hand and I will become a wife. I am old enough to hear a scary story."

Grandfather smiled and affectionately ruffled the hair under my hood. "So you are, little mother. I was almost forgetting."

He leaned back in his chair, his hands continuing to rasp slowly over the stone as he sanded away the roughness, leaving a delicate sheen in its place.

"Very well then," he said after a long silence when the only sound was the soft bubbling of the cooking pot. Then he told the following tale.

The stories of the old people, they seem like dreams to me. I do not know them well. But this one has stayed with me while many others fade from my mind. It concerns the man Atungaq and his wife, who traveled and traveled from one place to the next, leaving their little son and daughter behind, because they sought to go all around the world.

Atungaq and his wife saw many strange places and met many people as they journeyed. But for all her desire to see new places, the wife was always stricken with a paralyzing shyness when they came upon a new people. She claimed to be snow blind—even in the dead of winter when the sun did not rise—so that she did not have to talk with anyone. This ploy of the wife was met with sympathy when they traveled in the summer, but in the winter, the people they met laughed at her because they knew that she was lying.

After much journeying, another child was born to Atungaq and his wife; a little son whom they named for her father, who had visited her in a dream just prior to the boy's birth. The little one traveled with his parents, sleeping happily in the fur-lined pack at the back of his mother's parka.

Then one day, Atungaq and his wife were caught out in a great snowstorm. The dogs pulled and pulled the sled as hard as they could, fighting the great winds and driving snow, but they were tiring. Then Atungaq saw a snow-house ahead of them. It promised shelter from the storm and a place to rest his dogs. As he pulled the sled to a halt in front of the entrance, a woman came out to greet them and hastened them in out of the blizzard.

While Atungaq attended to his dogs, the wife and babe crawled through the tunnel into the snow house. Eagerly, the strange woman took the baby from the wife to allow her time to clear the snow from her parka. Suddenly, the babe gave a wail of pain, and the wife turned. To her horror, she saw that the evil spirit in the form of a woman had thrust a needle into the infant's head, killing it instantly. The baby's blood spilled everywhere as the wife screamed. Ignoring her, the evil creature placed its mouth on the wound to suck the blood from the child.

Then Atungaq burst through the tunnel, his eyes wild as he searched for the cause of his wife's scream. In an instant he saw the evil woman holding the murdered child and knew her for what she was: a Tammatuyuq. Realizing there was nothing he

TAMMATUYUQ

could do for his boy and knowing they were in great danger themselves from this demon, Atungaq grabbed hold of his hysterical wife and pulled her out of the snow house and back into the storm. Fortunately, he had barely begun unhitching the dogs from the sleigh when he heard his wife scream, so it took only a moment to put the harness back on the lead dog before they were on their way.

Behind them, through the howl of the storm, Atungaq thought he heard, just faintly, the sound of a frustrated scream when the Tammatuyuq realized her other victims had gotten away. He did not turn back to look, knowing that not even a Tammatuyuq would pursue them in such a storm.

As soon as he felt it was safe, Atungaq stopped the sled and made a shelter for them to hide in until the storm had passed. But his wife's spirit was wounded by the terrible encounter and the loss of her child, and so Atungaq stopped his wandering and took her home to her other children, who had grown to adulthood while their parents were away.

My grandfather stopped speaking and held his carving up to the seal-oil lamp to inspect it. I could not speak. My heart was pounding hard with fear of the Tammatuyuq and horror over the fate of the baby. But I had told my grandfather I was old enough to hear an adult story, and so I forced myself to breathe deeply until the pulse throbbing in my neck had calmed and my hands had stopped shaking.

Sensing that I had settled, Grandfather ceased his inspection of the stone figures and resumed his sanding. "There have been no reports of Tammatuyuq in many years," he said quietly. "Not since the old days. But we still tell the tale of Atungaq to remind us that these evil creatures once existed, so we will recognize them if the need arises."

I nodded my head soberly, understanding his warning. Better to be prepared than to be caught unawares.

"Thank you for telling me the story, Grandfather," I said, proud that my voice sounded so calm.

"Next time I will tell you a funny one," my Grandfather promised, and I grinned at him in relief as my mother and father came through the tunnel into the ice house. Their presence broke the storytelling spell my grandfather had woven, and I turned gratefully back to the real world, knowing that the time for tales was over for the day.

The Talking Head

SAULT SAINTE MARIE, ONTARIO

There once lived in the deep north a hunter who was so devoted to his trade that he was almost never home with his wife and two sons. The hunter had not chosen wisely when he took a wife, and his head was so full of the chase and the kill that he did not notice that she was fretful and nagging and completely unfaithful to him. All day long, the wife would talk, talk, talk to her sons and yak, yak, yak with the neighbors and nag, nag, nag at her husband when he came home for a precious few minutes at the end of the hunt.

The unfaithful wife had a series of male "friends" who came to visit her at the lodge, and she instructed her young boys never to speak of these men to their father. At first, the boys were too little to understand what was going on. But as they grew older, they became both horrified and embarrassed by their mother's outrageous behavior.

"I am tired of her talking and nagging and complaining," the elder boy said to his brother. "I am going to speak to father about her behavior." And his younger brother agreed.

That night, when the hunter came home, his eldest boy

took him aside while the unfaithful wife was outside talking loudly with her neighbor, and told him the whole story. When the wife returned to the lodge, her nagging voice preceding her by several yards, the hunter confronted her in righteous indignation and struck her dead where she stood.

And that was the end of that. The boy's paternal aunt came to live with them, and things at the lodge became peaceful for about a fortnight. Then their mother returned. Her voice woke the hunter and his boys in the middle of the night. Even before the mother's spirit materialized, they could hear her talk, talk, talking away as fast as she could. Moments later, she was standing at the center of the lodge, shaking her hand at the pretty young aunt who was caring for her sons.

The aunt trembled near the door as the glowing figure of the wife began to nag, nag, nag about the cleanliness of the lodge, the shoddy way she dressed the boys, the shameful condition of the blankets and dishes. The ghost went on and on until the hunter was forced to leave the lodge just to get enough sleep to hunt on the morrow. The boys and their aunt were not so lucky; they had to endure the ghostly mother's presence until the spirit grew bored and went to visit the neighbor's lodge.

Each night, the spirit of the mother would returned to talk, talk, talk to her sons and yak, yak, yak with the neighbors and nag, nag, nag at her husband and the aunt. It was hard to believe, but she was actually worse in death than she had been in life, and she became a source of intense irritation to the whole village. Nothing the hunter tried could rid his lodge of her incessant, prattling presence. Even the local medicine man

THE TALKING HEAD

gave up after unsuccessfully attempting to exorcise their village of her tiresome spirit.

Finally, everyone in the village packed up their belongings and left. The medicine man nicely but firmly told the hunter and his boys to move somewhere far away from the tribe and to take the spirit with them. The pretty young aunt patted each of them on the hand and then departed with the medicine man, who had decided a virtuous woman that could put up for so long with such a tiresome spirit was good material for a wife.

The hunter and his sons went south, hoping to leave the unwelcome spirit of the yakkety-yakking mother far behind. After traveling for many hours, the hunter left the boys to rest beside a large waterfall while he tracked down some game for their evening meal. The boys stood watching the flight of a beautiful crane that was riding on the surface of the whirling, eddying water at the bottom of the falls. Suddenly, they heard a thump, thump, thumping noise coming from behind them. They turned and saw the grisly remains of their mother's head rolling toward them, her nag, nag, nagging voice shouting loudly to be heard over the noise of the waterfall.

The younger boy stared in terror at the horrible, decaying head and then shouted down toward the crane: "Grandfather! Grandfather! We are being persecuted by a terrible spirit! Please take us across the falls."

The beautiful crane looked up from its play. Seeing their predicament, it flew up to the boys and landed beside them.

"Cling to my back," it told them, "but do not touch my head." The boys nodded obediently, and the crane took them up on its back and flew them across to the far shore.

The head of the dead mother screamed with outrage and nag, nag, nagged at the crane to take it across to her sons. "Come, grandfather," the talking head shouted. "Carry me across the waterfall to my poor, lost children!"

Across the river, the boys watched with apprehension as the crane flew to the grisly, rotting head and said, "Cling to my back, but do not touch my head." The mother's head promised obedience and the crane lifted it up from the ground. But the mother's spirit was as indiscreet in death as it had been in life. It was curious to know why the crane did not want its head touched. When they were about halfway across the waterfall, it bumped itself forward and tapped the crane on the head. Immediately, the crane twisted and lurched in distress and the head tumbled off its back and fell screaming into the roaring water below.

The head was swept against the sharp rocks, and the rotting brains burst forth from the demolished skull and flew out over the water. The crane banked and flew down toward the battered remains of the mother's head. "You were useless in life," it cried loudly. "You will not be useless in death! Become fish."

Immediately, the horrid, floating pieces of brain transformed into fish eggs, which, when hatched, grew into a delicate, flavorful whitefish that became very popular in the region. Thus the nag, nag, nagging spirit was destroyed forever, and the young boys were rescued from persecution.

When the hunter, upon his return, heard the boys' terrifying tale, he praised crafty grandfather crane and adopted it as his family totem. The hunter and his sons settled down in the place that became known as Sault Sainte Marie, and their descendants became great hunters and fishermen who ate numerous whitefish and always rejoiced in the flight of the crane.

The Dwarf's House

HUDSON BAY, NUNAVUT

I lurked under the table in the ice house, hiding from my mother, who was preparing to leave the house to visit my sister Nayummi, who had recently been married. I didn't want to go with her. I wanted to stay here with Grandfather, who had been working on a very interesting carving all day long. I wanted to look at the carving and see if Grandfather would tell me its story. But not with mother around. I wanted it to be just us men.

"Would you watch Amorak for me, Father?" Mother asked, glancing indulgently toward the table. I covered my mouth with my caribou-skin mitten to keep from giggling. She'd known where I was all along!

"I would," he replied gravely, setting his carving down on the floor of the snow house and beckoning to me. "Come here, young man."

I crawled out from under the table and ran to him with a laugh as Mother's feet disappeared into the tunnel leading to the outside world. Moonlight shone brightly through the ice window above us, illuminating Grandfather's face much more brilliantly than the seal-oil lamp hanging from the ceiling.

I flung myself against his knees. "Story!" I demanded. "Story!"

He grinned and hauled me onto his lap. "What story do you want to hear, little uncle?" he asked. (I was named for my grandfather's father's brother, and my mother said I had inherited his proud spirit and mischievous ways.)

"That one," I said, pointing my finger to the new carving sitting on the floor.

"So, you've been wondering about the dwarf," said Grandfather with a chuckle. He picked up the carving, which showed a snow house divided down the middle with a wall. On one side were two Inuit woman looking scared and clutching one another. On the other was a tiny little man tugging on the front end of a huge seal.

"This is the story of the Dwarf's house," my Grandfather began, and I settled back against his shoulder with a happy sigh to listen.

The Dwarf lived with his wife in a small ice house by the Arctic sea, and he spent much of his time fishing and trapping to provide the two of them with enough food to last through the Long Night. One day, he came home to some news. Two very tall Inuit women—a mother and daughter—had moved into the vacant ice house that stood right next door to the Dwarf's home and shared with it an inner wall.

The Dwarf's little wife was very shy and had not gone to greet the tall women. She never knew what to say to strangers

THE DWARF'S HOUSE

and was a little afraid of these new neighbors. The Dwarf, for his part, was rather annoyed. He preferred solitude, which is why he and his wife lived far away from the Dwarf village. Now, here came two noisy strangers to interrupt his meditations.

Thereafter, the muffled sound of thumping and the occasional raised voice would drift to the Dwarf and his wife through the common wall. Every time he heard the tall women, the Dwarf would glare at the wall and mutter darkly to himself about moving away. But the hunting and fishing were good at this location, so he never did.

The women in the neighboring ice house had no idea that the Dwarf and his wife lived next door to them. The Dwarf's home lay deep beneath the surface, and only the smallest hole indicated where the entrance might be. The women thought the thumping and soft buzz of voices they sometimes heard was just the shifting and grinding of the ice.

The daughter was frequently away from the ice house, for it was she who fished and hunted game for their survival. The old mother kept the *iglu* neat and clean, repaired their clothes, and cooked the meals. If the old woman sometimes found it strange that she smelled roasting fish when she herself was cooking caribou meat, she put it down to old age, not knowing the little Dwarf wife was right next door cooking too!

One day, shortly after the daughter came home from her fishing, the Dwarf managed to catch a huge prize. A bearded seal twice his size fell to his hunting skills, and he slowly dragged it toward his home in triumph. His Dwarf wife would be ecstatic when she saw his trophy and would fall upon his neck with hugs and nose rubs. He couldn't wait to see her face when she saw this huge creature of the sea!

The Dwarf decided to surprise her by bringing the seal inside the snow house where his tiny wife was sewing garments for their new baby, who was due to arrive soon. He hauled the huge beast to the tiny entrance to their ice house and dropped it onto the snow. Entering the house backwards, he pulled on the front end and the dead seal followed him inside. But the creature was too round about the belly to fit through the hole.

BOOM!

The ice house rang with a thundering crash as the seal smashed against the wall of ice around the entrance hole and refused to go any further.

BOOM!

The sound thundered out again as the Dwarf tugged at the recalcitrant seal.

Inside the Dwarf house, the little wife was watching her husband and the huge seal with wide, round eyes. Where had he gotten such a feast? And how were they ever going to get it inside the house?

In the adjacent ice house, the two tall women leapt to their feet in shock when they heard the loud booming.

"What is that sound?" cried the daughter.

"Aiy! It is an evil Tunnituaqruk!" the mother wailed. "The bad people with the tattooed faces of which the old ones spoke."

BOOM!

The sound came again, followed by some creative cursing through the wall.

"They have come for us! Flee!" shouted the mother, scrambling toward the entrance tunnel.

BOOM!

The whole ice house shook as the mother started to crawl through the ice tunnel. The daughter caught her by her boots and pulled her back inside.

"Mother, what if they are out there now, trying to get us to come out!" the daughter wailed in fear. "They would eat us!"

BOOM!

The shuddering bang came a fifth time, and the two women clung together in fear and alarm. Then the sound stopped. The mother and daughter stared at each other. Why had the evil ones stopped their pounding? Had they gone away?

The daughter grabbed her hunting spear and went outside to investigate.

In the adjacent ice house, the Dwarf gave up the idea of *pulling* the huge seal inside the house. He shoved it back outside, squeezed past it, and started pushing the seal from behind, just as the daughter emerged from the neighboring house.

The daughter stared pop-eyed at her tiny neighbor as he shoved frantically at the large bearded seal.

"Don't just stand there! Help me!" the Dwarf panted.

The daughter blinked a few times in surprise, dropped her spear, and went to help the Dwarf push the big seal through the hole.

BOOM!

The house shook as they shoved and pushed at the seal. Then, with a loud popping noise, the seal slid through the entrance and into the Dwarf's house.

The panting Dwarf stood up and surveyed his tall neighbor. Grudgingly, he decided she wasn't so bad after all and invited her and her mother to join them in a feast as soon as his little wife had cooked up a portion of the big seal.

The bemused daughter agreed and went to tell her mother all about the "evil Tunnituaqruk" who had turned out to be a Dwarf, and to break the news to her that they had neighbors sharing the wall of their ice house!

I giggled happily when Grandfather finished his tale, and I peered at the faces of the women in the carving. "Boom!" I cried happily. I slid off his lap and ran around and around the ice house joyfully. "Boom!"

"Boom!" replied my mother, sliding in through the entrance tunnel and catching me up in her arms. "I see Grandfather has been telling you stories again, little uncle!"

"About a dwarf!" I told her, as she nuzzled against me, rubbing my nose with hers. She laughed and hugged me close. "That was always my favorite story," she whispered in my ear.

"Me too!" I whispered back.

She put me back down on the floor, and Grandfather gave me the carving to play with while he and my mother spoke about adult things, as the moon set in the west and the darkness of the Long Night settled over our home.

25

The Lure

STANLEY PARK, VANCOUVER, BRITISH COLUMBIA

Many and many a long year ago, when the Squamish peopled this land, there lived an evil witch who plagued the good men and women living on the coast. Her bad medicine was powerful indeed, and there was not a clean soul that she did not long to destroy with her wickedness.

The witch-woman traveled from village to village, disguised as a wise woman, and would be welcomed with open arms. But soon after her arrival, the stout hearts of the brave warriors would falter for no reason. Their strong arms grew weak and they lost their ability to hunt. Children would be born with terrible deformities. The hearts of husbands and wives would turn against each other. Anger and suspicion and quarreling and strife inevitably fell upon any village in which the witch-woman dwelt, and it was soon followed by plagues and epidemics that would decimate the population. The witch-woman would laugh at her work and leave the village at the hour of its greatest need, when a true wise-woman would have attended the dying with her good medicine.

News of the witch-woman traveled up and down the coast,

and her evil spread in yet another way, for the friendly Squamish became hardened and suspicious of any stranger entering their villages for fear that he or she might be the witch-woman in disguise, come to wreck her bad medicine upon them. Pain and strife, suspicion and madness were meat and drink to the evil creature, and as they increased among the Squamish people, the witch-woman grew more powerful.

Sustained by her evil magic, the witch-woman outlived first her generation, and then the next. Always, she moved up and down the coast, entering into unwary homes and leaving chaos and terror and pain and death behind her. When a third generation was born, and still the witch-woman lived on to carry her bad medicine among them, the great Sagalie Tyee— the Squamish people's name for the Great Spirit—decided to put a stop to her evil once and for all.

Calling the Four Men, who were the Sagalie Tyee's representatives on Earth, he showed them the deeds of the evil witch-woman and instructed them to hunt her down and transform her into a solid stone that would harbor no growth. This was the harshest punishment he could devise for such an evil creature, for he knew he could not kill her and set her evil spirit free to roam wheresoever it willed.

The Four Men entered at once into their giant canoe and in the blink of an eye they were in the Narrows. As they paddled, they heard a wicked laugh come from the heights above them. The witch-woman was jeering at the Four Men from her precarious perch, daring them to catch her if they could. The Four Men beached the canoe at once and began climbing the rocks, but the witch-woman danced away from them, using her bad medicine to hide herself among the thickets and trees. She would dance in and out of sight like a will-'o-the-wisp, cursing and laughing alternately at the Four Men of the Sagalie Tyee.

"Take care, O Men of the Sagalie Tyee," she called from a thick tree branch above them. "Take care, or I will blight you with my evil eye." She vanished as soon as they saw her and reappeared farther away, dancing down a game trail mockingly.

Grimly, the Four Men followed the witch deeper and deeper into the sea-girt neck of land. In the thickest part of the woods, the witch-woman stumbled over a root and fell to her knees. Distracted by her fall, she allowed her spell to falter just a bit. This was enough to allow the tallest and mightiest of the Four Men to reach her with his good medicine.

Flinging out a giant arm, he pointed his finger at the witch-woman and cried: "Witch-woman of the stony heart, become stone forevermore, and bear a black stain upon your surface for every dark deed you have done!"

His spell hit the witch-woman as she was struggling to stand, and she screamed once in agony. Before their eyes, her body turned to a bare white stone, stained with many black marks that corroded its surface like the effects of a powerful acid. Everything near the stone shriveled and died instantly as the rock containing the chained soul of the evil witch settled against the ground, trapped forevermore in the depths of the sea-girt neck of land by the Narrows.

Even in her transformed state, the witch-woman still haunted the good people of the coast. Soon a powerful aura began emanating from the newly formed rock, acting as a lure

THE LURE

to draw in any human soul who wandered too close. Warriors and maidens, mothers and children fell one by one under the evil stone's spell. They would circle and circle in the woods around it, unable to find their way home. Minds maddened, willpower drained, and hope gone, the poor souls would eventually drop dead of exhaustion near the stone. But even death could not free them of the power of the witch-woman, and the trapped souls continued to circle the evil stone endlessly.

Seeing this new menace, the Sagalie Tyee had his Four Men search the world for the strongest, kindest, purest souls from among the human race. These brave people were transformed into magnificent trees and planted at the beginning of the game trail that led toward the stone. Such was the benevolent power and beauty of the new grove that all who came to the sea-girt neck of land were drawn to linger there and so escaped the power of the lure. Deprived of its victims, the evil spirit in the stone gradually fell asleep, and its power waned.

Today, the sea-girt neck of land is known as Stanley Park, and its magnificent trees are still enjoyed by millions. But somewhere in the woods sleeps a stone of great power. And those who walk its pathways must take care so as not to awaken the evil lure at the heart of Stanley Park.

26

Forerunner

MARION BRIDGE, NOVA SCOTIA

It all happened a long time ago, now, and we never talked about it much after the funeral, out of respect for the poor little mother who lost her child so tragically.

I was already a grandfather—howbeit only for one month—at the time the incident took place, but I was still doing a full day's work right alongside my two grown sons. My house was next door to the smithy, which is why I happen to know the whole story, not just the bits and pieces that floated around town.

It started with the blue light that appeared mysteriously on board a small boat up the river at Grand Mira. It was a bonny boat that was for sale by the owner, but not a man on the river would touch it because of the strange glow that appeared within it at night. Finally, the blacksmith, who was not a superstitious man, eschewed the rumors of a ghost, bought the boat, and brought it down to his place.

Sometimes, when I tramped home after dark, I would see the reflection of a blue light coming from the boat and I would stop to stare at it, my flesh crawling at the sight. The blacksmith was a braver man than me! I wouldn't get in that boat if you paid me a day's wages. No sir!

A few evenings after I saw the blue light in the boat, one of the neighborhood ladies came over to borrow some baking pans from my wife, since her in-laws were coming to town and she wanted to make a special dessert. Naturally, the two friends lingered long over the task and finally settled at the table with steaming cups of tea to gossip about events in town. I sat near the woodstove, whittling on a wooden toy to give to my baby grandson and pretending not to listen to the ladies' talk.

I noticed that our neighbor was playing with her cup and saucer rather than drinking her tea. She obviously had something on her mind—something more than the prospective visit from the in-laws—and she wasn't sure how to bring it up. Finally, she just blurted it out: "The strangest thing happened yesterday," she said, setting down her cup and clasping her hands tightly in her lap.

"What was it?" asked my wife, her eyes widening a little at her friend's obvious tension.

"Little Neil and I were walking over the Marion Bridge last night," she said, swallowing nervously, "when he suddenly pulled away from my hand and ran to peer down into the water. He told me that he saw the body of a boy lying on the bottom of the river. But when I ran to look, there was nothing there."

My pulse throbbed suddenly in my wrists and neck. *Forerunner,* I thought, my body going cold. I'd heard many reports about forerunners through my long life. A fellow over in Amherst had gone to shut his bedroom door one night after

FORERUNNER

it blew open in the wind and saw the body of his wife all pale and cold, floating in the air in front of him even though he could hear her snoring in the bed behind. She took sick the next day and died a week later.

Then there was the chap near Forchu who moved into a fishing shack out on the point and started hearing men screaming in agony night after night, though no one else was there. His nerve broke after a few nights, and he moved away. Shortly after he was gone, a ship went down in a storm right at that spot. None of the residents could rescue the sailors because the wind and the waves were so fierce, and they were forced to watch as one by one the fearful and maddened men dropped from the masts to their death with shrieks of agony, just like those described by the chap who'd been staying in the nearby fishing hut.

My wife was saying something soothing to our neighbor about children's imaginations as I brought my mind back to the conversation. Slowly her friend relaxed her tightly gripped hands and once again took up her teacup, comforted by my wife's words and tone. But I was not comforted and stared sightlessly into the grate of the stove, wondering bleakly who it was that was destined to die. In a small town, you knew everyone, and everyone knows you. The potential loss of one of our young people was too frightening to contemplate.

I managed to put the incident out of my mind by dint of some good hard work the next day and didn't think of it again until a few nights later when I was awakened by a great clattering sound from the smithy. I ran to the open window and looked out, but I could see nothing until the blacksmith appeared with a lantern and a scowling countenance. I raced out of the house to join him, and we entered the building together. Before our astonished eyes, we saw the grappling iron dancing across the table, making a tremendous racket as it jarred the other implements of my friend's trade. The iron gave one or two leaps as the lantern light hit it, then fell to the floor with a clatter and stopped moving.

"Tell me I'm not dreaming," the blacksmith gasped, the light quivering around us as the lantern shook in his grasp.

"If you are, then so am I," I told him grimly. Biting my lip to get up my courage, I stormed forward, picked up the errant grappling hook, and returned it to its proper place. Behind me, the shaking blacksmith straightened the tools on the table. Then we went back out into the night and shut the door firmly behind us. For some reason, I kept thinking about the blue light and the vision our neighbor's son had at the bridge, and my heart was filled with dread.

I must have slept badly after the incident, for when I woke, my back was so sore I could hardly stand up. My wife made me stay home from work that morning and coddled me as if I were a baby. I'm ashamed to admit I enjoyed every minute of it.

I slept the morning away, and by early afternoon my back was feeling a touch better. I sat up in bed, carefully stood up, and eased my way downstairs, listening absently to the cheerful voice of a little village lad named Sandy Munro as he chatted merrily to the blacksmith. The little lad haunted the smithy. It was his favorite place to play, and he often ran errands for the men working there. The blacksmith was arranging for the boy to take an axe across the bridge for him; a task to which the happy fellow instantly agreed.

My wife was out doing some shopping. She came in a few minutes later, shaking her head angrily. When I inquired as to the reason for her ire, she sputtered: "Those two bad boys were bullying little Sandy just now out by the bridge over some axe he was carting about for the blacksmith! I've half a mind to go out there and box their ears!"

I knew instantly who she meant. There was a widow in town who'd earned a reputation as a witch, and her two sons tended to bully all the schoolchildren.

"Do you want me to go talk to them?" I asked, trying to rise from my chair. My wife made a scolding noise and pushed me back into the seat. "I'll go," she said, whisking out the door before I could utter another word. She came back a moment later.

"They're gone now, more's the pity," she said. "I am going to speak to their mother. They're going to hurt someone one of these days!"

I nodded grimly. Yes, it was time something was done about those rascals.

I dozed for the rest of the afternoon next to the warm woodstove and woke at suppertime to the sound of alarmed shouts and a great deal of clamor outside. By the time I'd gotten my sore back out of the chair and hobbled down the steps, the blacksmith and his son were out on the river in his new boat.

In his huge calloused hands, the blacksmith carried the grappling iron that had made such a racket the previous night. And he used it to pull the body of a boy from the bottom of the river, right where our neighbor's son had seen it in his vision. It was little Sandy.

The child's body was laid out on the bridge of the boat—right where the blue light had so often appeared—and a crowd gathered to see him. His poor mother was so distraught that she had to be led away by my wife. I remained where I was, staring in horror at the poor little boy with the blood-clotted wound on his head. Not being a doctor, I had no way of knowing if it was the blow to the head that killed him, or if he had merely been stunned and had drowned. But it didn't matter. What mattered was that a little life had been snuffed out. And in the back of my mind, I wondered what had happened to the blacksmith's axe that the little fellow had been carrying.

At that moment, the two bad boys my wife had seen arguing with little Sandy on the bridge came sauntering up to look at the body. I watched one of the lads approach the child, and as he stepped up to the boat, the wound on Sandy's head began to bleed freely, as if he were still alive. I gasped softly, and the bully's eyes widened at the sight. He hurriedly backed away from the corpse and went to stand beside his brother. As soon as he moved away from the boat, the bleeding stopped.

Anxiously, the bully grabbed his brother's arm, and they hurried away. I watched them go, remembering the old stories my grandmother had told us as children about murdered corpses that bled when their killer passed by. But of course, there was no way to prove anything. No way at all.

The whole town turned out for the funeral, and my wife and I supported and comforted Miz Munro as best we could in the days that followed. She confided in us shortly after the funeral that her son had appeared to her in a dream the night after his death. Taking her to the blacksmith's shop and pointing to the empty slot where the smith's axe usually hung, he said: "That is the axe that killed me." Then he told her the name of his murderer. It was the boy who had approached the boat and made the corpse bleed.

The story spread quickly around town but was hushed up, since there was no way to prove the child's death was anything but an accident. The witch-woman and her two sons moved away shortly after the funeral and were never heard from again. And no one ever found the blacksmith's missing axe.

Well, as I said in the beginning, it all happened a long time ago, now, and we never talk about it much. But I've always believed in forerunners ever since that fateful day. And I'm glad those bullies left town before my grandson reached school age—even though it was too late for poor little Sandy.

27

The Skeleton

FORT MCLEOD, ALBERTA

The chief was frustrated and disgusted. He'd taken a group of warriors with him in what should have been a surprise attack on an enemy camp, only to find his adversaries armed and wary. A spy had obviously observed their departure from camp and reported it to the enemy.

The chief pulled back his men immediately, for he was a good leader and did not want unnecessary harm to come to them. But calling off the attack left him both angry and embarrassed.

Abruptly, he wheeled his horse to the side of his wife's brother, who was one of the war party, and said: "Take the men down to the Belly River and make camp there. I go to kill a buffalo and meditate. I will come to you when my task is complete."

His wife's brother nodded. The two men had long been friends, and he realized at once that the chief wished to regain his composure before returning to the tribe. The warriors turned back, taking the chief's horse with them, and he proceeded alone. It did not take him long to fall upon the tracks of a small herd, and soon he had stalked and killed a buffalo.

The familiar act of meditating and hunting a buffalo soothed the chief's irritation. After carefully packing away all the buffalo meat he could carry, he turned and walked for about an hour before making a rough camp and roasting some of the meat for his supper. As the delicious scent of his meal wafted to his nose, the chief's eyes went to his gun, and a stray thought came to him.

"If only I had remembered to take some hair from that buffalo's head, I might have been able to clean my gun," he muttered aloud, annoyed with himself for not thinking of this sooner.

No sooner had the words left his lips than he was touched by a chill breeze that swirled around his face and shoulders, and then away. A moment later, a shag of buffalo hair blew toward him and fell right at his feet. The chief stared at the hair, completely nonplussed. He shivered superstitiously and turned back to the fire without touching the shag. He hurriedly removed his dinner and dashed out the flames, wanting to get away from this haunted place immediately.

He ate the roasted meat as he walked through the gathering dusk, crossing a stream and making his way to the river. Deciding he'd put a safe distance between himself and whatever haunted that particular hillock, he found a patch of rye grass that looked fairly comfortable and settled himself down to sleep.

When he woke at dawn, he found himself curled up next to the skeleton of a woman. It had desiccated down to the bones, but there was enough of her dress left to identify her as a Blackfoot. He gave a gasp of horror and rolled away, his heart thumping madly with shock. Leaping to his feet, the chief paused only long enough to grab pack and gun and then ran along the game trail in the direction his warriors had taken the previous day.

The chief slowed finally, and then settled down into a half-jogging pace that he could keep up all day. He couldn't shake the feeling that something was following him, though when he paused to search for an adversary in the surrounding woods, he found none. Apprehension drove him onward past his normal capacities, so that he reached the Belly River by nightfall.

Exhausted, the chief made camp in the lee of a fallen tree and built a small fire. As his meal was roasting, he heard a soft whistling sound coming from the upper reaches of the fallen tree. He whirled in alarm and saw the skeleton of the Blackfoot woman sitting astride a branch, swinging its legs in time to its whistle and gazing up at the stars.

An icy wave of shock pulsed once through the chief's body, and he reeled back from the sight. "Go away, I beg you," he cried. The skeleton gave him a toothy smile and then continued her whistling. She broke off to say: "Why didn't you accept the buffalo hair I sent you, husband?"

"I am not your husband," the chief snapped, his whole body cringing at the notion.

"Of course you are," said the skeleton. "I picked you to be my husband when you stopped to roast a buffalo on my grave. *Here is a fine warrior*, I thought, and so I left my place of rest to follow you."

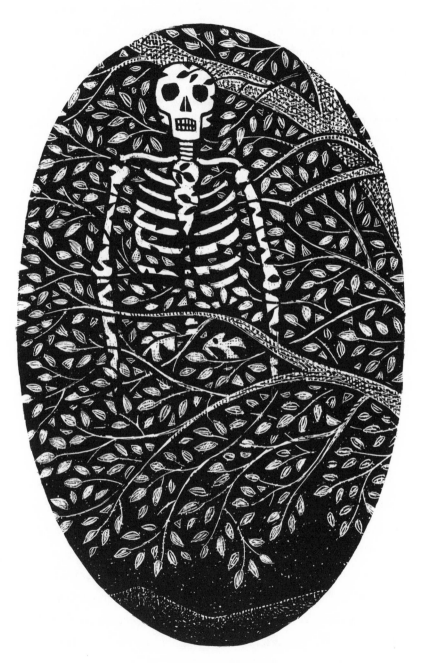

THE SKELETON

"I already have a wife and I want no other," the chief said, unable to tear his eyes from the gruesome, half-decomposed woman sitting on the branch above him. "Go away."

"No," said the skeleton, and turned her gaze back up to the stars. She started whistling again as the chief turned his back on her (not without feeling a shiver of fear run down his spine) and grimly retrieved his meat from the fire before it burned to a crisp.

"Smells good," said the skeleton. "May I have some?"

"No!" roared the chief, irritation overriding his fear. "Go away."

"You are a cruel husband," remarked the skeleton complacently.

"I am not your husband!" shouted the chief. "Go away!"

Grabbing up rifle, he fired a few shots right into the dried-out figure astride the tree branch.

The skeleton clutched its chest dramatically as it fell from the branch. "You have killed me again!" she screamed. "Dog! Faithless husband! There is nowhere you can hide from me now."

Her shriek echoed and re-echoed through the woods, growing louder and louder until the chief's ears rang. Hastily dumping river water on the fire, the chief fled from the cursed spot, pack bumping against his trembling legs and gun heavy in his hand.

Gradually, the skeleton's shrieks faded away, but when the chief stopped to rest, he could hear the creature running through the trees toward him and could even make out the sound of her cursing. Frightened anew, he fled through the darkness, careless of what tracks he might be leaving. To get away was his only thought.

The chief caught a few minutes' rest here and there, when the sound of the skeleton died briefly away. He was aiming for the buttes where his warriors typically made camp. If he could reach them, then together they might drive the foul spirit away.

As he raced through the final leg of his journey, the sky lightened with the dawn, and he could see his camp ahead of him. Behind him, he could hear the skeleton chiding and cursing him. It seemed to be gaining on him, so the chief put on a final burst of speed, stumbling forward on burning legs, his lungs filled with fire. He could no longer run and barely had the strength or dignity left to stay upright.

A few of his warriors spotted him and came racing down to meet him.

"Chief, you had best not let your wife's brother see that woman you brought back with you. He will not like your having taken a second wife," one of the men warned in a low tone when he reached his chief.

"I have taken no other wife," the chief panted. "It is a foul spirit that haunts me."

The warriors exchanged puzzled glances, but when they looked back toward the river, the figure following their chief had disappeared. Two men were dispatched to track the skeleton, and the others escorted their chief into camp. The trackers returned after an hour with disturbing news. The only footprints they could find along the trail were those of their chief. And yet all the men had seen the second figure following him through the early light of dawn.

The men hurriedly packed up their camp, mounted their horses, and headed for home, hoping to leave the fey skeleton that haunted their chief behind with their speed. When they reached their village, the warriors were greeted with cheers and welcome fires burned at every lodge. A large feast had been prepared at the center of the village.

The chief ducked into his lodge and held his wife close, whispering to her of the terrible thing that had befallen him on the return journey.

"You should have brought the skeleton-woman home," his wife said teasingly. "She could have taken over all the mending!" As she hoped, her banter made the chief smile, and he felt as if a burden had lifted from him. He hugged her close again. Oh, he had chosen the very best of wives. No ghostly skeleton could ever compare with her!

"Come now," his wife said. "We eat with my brother and his family. Let us feast to your return."

The chief nodded enthusiastically, suddenly hungry now that the weight of fear had fallen from him. As they left their tepee, the chief saw a black bear ambling out of the brush at the edge of camp. The creature was obviously attracted by the smell of the feast. Picking up a bone that was lying outside his tent, the chief hurled it at the bear, hoping to discourage it from entering the camp.

"Again you try to kill me," the bear shrieked aloud with the voice of the skeleton-woman. The chief's eyes bulged, and beside him his wife screamed in terror. Before their eyes, the bear slowly transformed into the skeleton husk of the Blackfoot woman. Around the great fire at the center of camp, all the people turned to stare when they heard the screaming, and great was their consternation when they saw the skeleton.

"An evil ghost is upon us!" the chief shouted. "Into my lodge! Now!"

There was a general stampede toward the large lodge at the center of the village. Within moments, every soul that lived in the camp was crammed into the chief's tepee. Outside, they heard the skeleton tramping about, shrieking and grumbling and smashing against the sides of the lodge with its hands. An unnatural wind sprang up and blew the smoke from the chief's hearth back into the tepee so that everyone choked and coughed.

"We must appease the spirit," the chief's mother exclaimed suddenly. She pushed her way to the small fire that burned at the heart of the tepee and lit a fancy pipe that the chief's wife kept carefully stored for special occasions.

"Mother, what do you do?" asked the chief in alarm, as his only living parent shoved her way to the entrance of the tepee. To his horror, she called out to the skeleton: "I come to you with a gift" and then stepped out of the lodge.

"Mother!" the chief exclaimed, and sprang out after her. He saw the skeleton standing a few feet away, its eye sockets fixed on his mother.

"Come back into the lodge," the chief ordered, grabbing his mother to tug her back to safety. But he couldn't move her at all. She was stuck to the ground as if a supernatural weight held her down. Her eyes were fixed on the evil skeleton, which was slowly backing toward the woods. Step by step his mother followed it, as if pulled by an invincible power.

"Help me!" shouted the chief, wrapping his long arms around his mother's waist and pulling backward with all his might. But the tug of the skeleton was irresistible, and he found himself stumbling forward one step, then two. He felt his wife's arms around his waist, pulling him back. Out of the corner of his eye, he saw his wife's brother catch hold of her, and then the brother's wife take hold of him. Soon there was a human chain that stretched throughout the village, each person holding the one in front and pulling backward against the power of the spirit that entranced the chief's mother.

Suddenly, the chief's mother gave a terrible shriek, and the pipe fell from her hands. At the outskirts of the village, the skeleton laughed aloud.

"My vengeance is complete! Farewell, husband," the skeleton cried. Then it disappeared in a puff of acrid smoke. Within the circle of his arms, the chief's mother sagged. By the time he eased her to the ground, she was dead.

Appeased of its anger by the taking of an innocent life, the evil skeleton returned to its far-off resting place. But ever after, the grief-stricken chief and his men avoided the hunting ground near the river where the skeleton lay buried, for fear of arousing the evil spirit once again.

The Warning

OTTAWA, ONTARIO

I was assigned to the new Governor General's office in 1872, shortly after Lord Dufferin arrived in Canada, and quickly became his lordship's personal aide. I was impressed with Dufferin from the start. He had a knack for politics, and during his term of office, Prince Edward Island was admitted to the Confederation; the Supreme Court of Canada and the Royal Military College of Canada were established; and the Intercolonial Railway was completed.

Dufferin quickly proved himself at ease speaking with a wide variety of Canadians, both in English and French. Over the years, I observed him in many diverse situations: addressing the National Club in Toronto, speaking with residents of Icelandic settlements in Manitoba, lecturing at la Societé Saint-Jean-Baptiste de Montreal, and conversing with laborers in British Columbia. His easy manner and charm won him many followers from all walks of life, including my rather hard-to-please wife, who frequently waxed eloquent over his charm and hospitality.

Lord Dufferin concentrated on promoting Canadian unity

and made it his business to visit every Canadian province. Dufferin was also a firm believer in recognizing excellence among Canadians. In 1873, he established the Governor General's Academic Medals for superior academic achievement by Canadian students, and he also instituted several sporting prizes. Lord and Lady Dufferin organized numerous balls, concerts, dinners, theatrical performances, and receptions of all kinds—and Lady Dufferin loved to perform the lead role in the plays at Rideau Hall, the Governor General's official residence.

It soon became obvious that more room was needed at the hall, so the Lord and Lady added several extensions to it and built a skating rink, curling rink, and toboggan slide in 1872 and 1873 with their own money, though they were later reimbursed by the government. Their goal of attracting more Canadians to the Hall grounds was more than exceeded. My wife and I would sometimes sneak away from our official duties to skate together at the rink.

Lady Dufferin got involved too, attending many parliamentary debates and reporting all the happenings therein back to her husband. She maintained a high profile during her husband's term as Governor General, frequently appearing in public, and was the first spouse to accompany the Governor General on a tour. By the end of their term, she had visited every province with her husband. In fact, she and her husband were the first Governor General and consort to visit the province of Manitoba. During their trip, they each drove a spike in the line of what would become the Canadian Pacific Railway.

One evening, shortly after his return from Manitoba, Lord Dufferin and I retreated to his office for a drink following a long day of meetings. I could tell the Governor General was on edge about something. There was something brittle underneath the suave charm he usually displayed. I was wondering how to broach the subject when he brought it up himself.

"Do you believe in omens?" he asked, as he poured brandy into two glasses. I hesitated, not sure how to respond. I did believe in omens and in the second sight, which ran in my family on my mother's side.

"Yes, I do," I admitted cautiously. "In my mother's family, a blue ball of light hovers on the family grounds in Scotland the night before a relative dies. It has been recorded for more generations than I can count."

To my relief, Lord Dufferin nodded as he handed me a glass. He took a seat beside the fire and sat sipping his drink thoughtfully, allowing the silence to lengthen. Then he sighed and looked over at me.

"Two or perhaps three times in my life, I have had a dream," he said. "Perhaps it would better be classified a nightmare. It is always the same. I am standing at my bedroom window at midnight, and a coffin appears on the horizon and slowly floats toward me. Somehow I know that it is mine, and that death approaches me. In the vision, I back away from the window and shut my eyes. When I open them, the coffin is gone."

I shuddered sympathetically and took another sip of brandy. My grandmother would call that dream a bad omen. And I would have to agree with her.

"And you had the dream again last night?" I asked, when the silence went on too long for comfort. He nodded, staring into the fire.

"Only this time, it was different," Dufferin said. "When the coffin appeared on the horizon, it was being dragged by an ominous, dark-clad figure. I could not make out any of the man's features, and as usual, my dream self instantly backed away and closed its eyes. When I opened them again, coffin and dark figure had vanished."

He swallowed the last of his drink and got up to pour himself a second. "I think I am most disturbed by the change in the dream. It was always the same in the past. I wonder if the change signals the imminent approach of death?"

His hand shook a little as he spoke, and some of the brandy splashed on the table. He swore softly and took out his handkerchief to wipe it up. Then he offered me a refill, which I accepted, and finally returned to sit again by the flickering flames at the hearth.

"It may not be a death omen," I suggested to my employer, who was also my friend. "Perhaps it is merely a warning. Something to keep you on your guard so that when the time comes, you can avoid a fatal incident."

Dufferin's eyes snapped to me, an arrested look upon his face. Obviously, this had never occurred to him before. "You could be right," he said slowly. As I watched, I saw the tension in his shoulders and arms relax as he accepted my words. "Yes, you may be right."

After a moment's contemplation, he turned the conversation to a discussion of the day's meetings, but just before I left, he asked me not to speak to anyone about what he had told me. Apparently, I was the only person in whom he had ever confided his recurring nightmare, and I felt privileged to be so trusted by a man whom I respected above all others.

Dufferin's term of office came to an end in 1878, and he moved on to other diplomatic duties. I remained in Ottawa, moving ever upward in my own career. Dufferin and I were frequent correspondents, and I often sought his counsel as I maneuvered my way through the politics surrounding my position.

A few years after his departure from Canada, I received an agitated letter from him. In it, he told me that he had seen the same vision once again—this time while he was awake. In it, a dark, sinister man had appeared before his eyes on the moon-bathed lawn of his country home, dragging a coffin behind him. This time, the face and figure of the man were quite clear, and Dufferin's description was detailed. He closed the letter by saying: "I would know this man if I ever saw him in person. I do not know if it is a real man or just some foul creature of portent. If your theory is correct, then he may be a real man. If I see him, I will avoid him at all costs."

"I should hope so," I muttered to myself as I folded the letter and filed it away with the others.

The years passed by with speed, and soon I was writing to my friend about the antics of my grandchildren. Dufferin's career had taken him many places during that time: Moscow, New Delhi, Rome. Now he was serving as an ambassador in Paris, France, and he would kindly enclose drawings for my wife of the latest fashions in each of his letters. Consequently, my wife was a fashion leader in Ottawa. People always wondered how she knew what was coming long before anyone else, but we never told them her secret.

THE WARNING

One morning, an express letter arrived from Paris. I was astonished. What could be so pressing that Dufferin would send the news express? I instructed my assistant that I was not to be disturbed and then took the letter into my office to read. It was short and to the point.

On the day prior to the writing of the letter, Dufferin had been in the Grand Hotel in Paris. He had walked through the foyer and summoned the lift. When the doors opened, he stepped inside and turned to look at the lift operator. It was the man he had seen in his vision!

With a gasp, Dufferin leapt out of the lift before its doors could close behind him. Trembling, he found a secluded corner in which to calm himself. His eyes kept returning to the lift, which climbed upwards floor by floor, until it reached the fifth.

The lift paused at the fifth floor for several long moments. Then the hotel was filled with the metallic twanging of breaking cables, and the elevator came roaring down the shaft with a sound like the wind. Dufferin could hear passengers screaming as they plummeted downward. Then the lobby was shaken floor to ceiling by the crash and screech of twisting metal as the lift slammed against the bottom of the shaft.

Spurred to action, Dufferin helped the hotel staff rescue the injured—one of whom was the newly hired lift operator— and the bodies of the dead. The sight of the lift operator no longer held any fear for Dufferin, for he was convinced that the danger to himself had passed when he exited the lift just prior to the crash.

"I do not think I will be troubled by any more dreams or

visions," he concluded in his missive. "But I have you to thank for this tragedy averted. If you had not suggested that the dreams might be a warning rather than an omen, I would probably not have thought to leave when I recognized the lift operator as the man from my vision. Thank you, my friend. I believe that your words that long-ago night in Ottawa saved my life yesterday."

I was shaking myself by the time I finished the letter. What a close shave. If Lord Dufferin had not had his vision, he very well might have died in that lift. Slowly I folded the letter and tapped it on my palm. I wasn't sure if it was true that my words had saved his life. He probably would have fled anyway as soon as he saw the lift operator's face. But I was pleased that he found my long-ago counsel as useful to him as I found his words of wisdom useful to me.

After that day, I had a healthy respect for omens and never joined in when others derided them. I knew better.

Corpse Candle

We had a bit of free time after chores that day, so my buddy Bob and I were hanging around in the front yard of my house. We'd practiced some baseball, but gave that up when it got too dark and were just lying in the grass, watching the fireflies come out.

Suddenly, my eye was caught by a bobbing light coming down the road from the east. It looked like a lantern. I nudged Bob and pointed. He rolled over on the grass and peered vaguely down the dark lane.

"Well, now, that's probably Phillip come to visit now that chores are done," Bob said lazily. "Too bad he missed our practice. He could use a little help catching fly balls."

"Come on!" I said, jumping up and scattering the hovering fireflies. "Let's go meet him."

Bob gave a moan of protest, rubbing a work-roughened hand across his brown eyes and through his shaggy black hair. Then he followed me out the gate and down the lane toward the bobbing light. As we drew closer, it paused and then began to backtrack down the lane.

"Hello, Phillip! It's only us, Dan and Bob!" I called, picking up my pace. The light was about a hundred yards away at that point, and was retreating through the darkness at a steady pace. Bob clutched my arm suddenly, bringing me to a halt.

"Dan," he said, alarm in his voice. "That's not a lantern! There's no one holding that light!"

"Don't be ridiculous," I said crossly, trying to ignore the superstitious prickle crawling across my skin. I narrowed my eyes, trying to get a better look at the light, which had stopped moving and was bobbing up and then down about a hundred yards away. And I saw then that he was right. It was just a blue-white glow suspended in midair. No Phillip. No lantern. Just a light.

A shudder went through my body, and I felt my eyes popping right out of my head in shock and fear. As I stared at it, the light bobbed closer, backed away, and bobbed closer again.

"It wants us to follow it," Bob said, an urgent note creeping into his voice. "Come on!"

Now Bob was ahead of me, following the bobbing light. It kept zigzagging this way and that, but it was leading us in the general direction of Bob's house. I kept swallowing as we jogged along, trying to bite back the bile that rose in my throat from the violent fear churning in my stomach. What was this strange light? Why had it summoned us?

After about ten minutes, we turned a corner and could clearly see Bob's house in the distance. As we sped along, the light went ahead of us and settled on top of the log stable. Bob was really anxious, now. He raced right passed the stable with its mysterious decoration and burst into the house, with me at his heels. We stood panting in the rugged kitchen, and I braced myself against one of the chairs beside the broad table at its center.

At that moment, Lizzie, Bob's middle sister, came racing down the stairs, her face white and tight with anxiety. As soon as she saw Bob, she flung herself into his arms and sobbed out something incoherent. Bob patted her on the back and tried to calm her down enough so that he could make out what she was saying. I watched in envy. I had a bit of a crush on Lizzie and wouldn't have minded comforting her myself.

"Sarah is ill. Very ill," Lizzie managed to gasp out, emerging from her brother's embrace. "You've got to go for the doctor, Bob. At once! Father still hasn't returned from the meeting in Regina. We think he missed the train and won't get back until sometime tomorrow."

Bob's face went grim. Sarah was his baby sister, just ten years old. "Come on, Dan," he said gruffly. "Let's fetch the doc."

Lizzie blinked and turned around, seeing me for the first time. Her hand went automatically to straighten her curly blond hair, and she gave me a shy smile that set my pulse pounding with something other than fear. "Thank you, Dan, for helping us," she said, blushing.

Bob took no notice of this exchange. He sent Lizzie back upstairs to help tend to Sarah and hustled me out to the log stable, which was still adorned with the phantom light. We hitched the horse to his father's buckboard as quickly as we could and made the nine miles into town in record time.

Fortunately for us, the doctor was home. He grabbed his

CORPSE CANDLE

black bag and jumped into the buckboard beside Bob, while I leapt into the back. None of us spoke much on the return journey, which was—if anything—faster than before. As we approached the farm, I saw that the ghost light still perched atop the stable, and I felt a throb of fear. Lizzie had been terrified for her sister's life. What if we were too late?

Bob threw the reins to me as he pulled the running horse to a halt. He and the doctor were out of the buckboard and into the house before the wagon had stopped moving. I unhitched the trembling horse and tended to her carefully, for she had done the family a great service this night. Then I put the buckboard away. I took my time, not wanting to intrude upon a family crisis any more than was proper.

As I came out of the log stable, I looked up at the roof and saw the light hovering above it. It was a dainty light, with faint blue tints to it, and at this distance, it looked like the flame of a candle. Suddenly, the flame blazed, getting brighter and brighter, and for a moment I saw the face of little Sarah at its center. Then it winked out and there was only darkness.

Through the open upstairs window of the house, I heard Bob's mother give a sudden cry of anguish, and then there was the sound of disconsolate sobbing. I knew then that little Sarah was dead.

I waited silently for the doctor and Bob in the kitchen. When they came downstairs at last, I gave my grieving friend a rough hug and told the family that I would take the doctor home in my carriage. Doc and I walked the ten minutes back to my place, and he helped me hitch up the family horse. While we drove into town, I told him about the mysterious light that Bob and I had followed. Doc nodded wearily, his rugged old face creased with sadness. "Yes, I have heard of that phenomenon," he said. "They're sometimes called corpse candles, and appear just prior to a death."

I shuddered a bit at his words, and he smiled sympathetically in the starlight.

"It's interesting that it came to fetch young Bob," said the doctor. "Perhaps Providence realized that Bob wouldn't be able to forgive himself if he wasn't given the chance to do all he could to save his little sister."

Knowing Bob, I thought that the doctor was probably right. I dropped him off at his house and then turned my horse toward home, riding slowly as I pondered the imponderable and grieved silently for Bob and his family over the death of his little sister Sarah.

Wendigo

A chill was in the air, heralding the approach of winter as the tribe gathered around the communal fire at the center of the village to celebrate a successful hunt. There was singing and laughing and dancing and some courting between the nubile young people at the outer fringes of the circle of light.

Toward the end of the evening, as voices got softer and bodies grew weary, Summer Moon, the oldest and wisest woman in the village, gave the soft shriek that heralded the onset of a vision. Instantly a hush fell over the villagers, and they crowded close as the old woman began to chant and sway. Slowly she rose and approached the fire, and when she reached its edge she spoke in a deep, sepulchral voice quite unlike her own light, merry tone. "It comes," she intoned. A ripple of fear ran through her audience when they heard her words. Suddenly, the shadows were no longer friendly, and the fire-light no longer comforted.

"It comes," Summer Moon intoned again. "It comes with the storm! It comes!" Her words ended in a terrible shriek. The villagers drew back, wives shrinking behind their warrior-husbands in fright and children huddling against their mothers' skirts. Only the chief dared face the frenzied wise woman.

"What comes, good mother?" he asked, with only the slightest tremble in his voice.

She turned eyes that glowed with silvery lights upon him. "Wendigo," she hissed, and the word seemed to echo unnaturally through the crisp autumn air. "Wendigo."

Summer Moon's eyes rolled up suddenly, showing their whites, and then she fainted, falling down right next to the bonfire. The chief ran forward, swept the old wise woman up in his arms, and carried her to her son's lodge. Behind him, the villagers broke out into terrified murmurs, the one word circling over and over throughout the camp. "Wendigo. Wendigo."

Young Moonflower, the granddaughter of Summer Moon and the most beautiful maiden in the village, clutched her elder brother's arm in fear. "What is a Wendigo?" she whispered to her beloved sibling. "Whenever I have asked Grandmother about it, she always changes the subject."

Grey Fox narrowed his eyes and studied the sweet face beside him. He and his sister were orphans. They had been raised by Summer Moon and their uncle Dancing Caribou, who was a widower, after their parents were killed in an accident when Grey Fox was ten and Moonflower only two. He had always protected his little sister and considered fobbing her off with a light answer. But Moonflower was almost a woman grown. Come the spring, suitors would be haunting his lodge, seeking her hand in marriage. She deserved the truth, and so he told her all he knew about the Wendigo.

According to the stories, it was a large creature, as tall as a tree, with a skeletal, deformed body, a lipless mouth, jagged teeth, and a heart made of pure ice. Its breath was a strange hiss, its footprints full of blood, and it ate any man, woman, or child who ventured into its territory. And those who it killed were the lucky ones. Sometimes, the spirit of the Wendigo chose to possess a person instead. The luckless individual then became a Wendigo himself, hunting down those he had once loved and feasting upon their flesh. No one in their village had ever been unfortunate enough to encounter a Wendigo. Up until now.

Moonflower's lovely golden-brown eyes grew large with fear as Grey Fox spoke of the evil spirit that was the Wendigo. "And it is coming here?" she whispered, her voice laced with fear. Unknowingly, her fingers dug painfully into the flesh of her brother's arm as she struggled to comprehend her grand-mother's message to the people of the village. Grey Fox removed her hand and clasped it warmly in his own. "Do not be afraid, little sister. I will protect you," he promised. She gazed up at him trustingly and nodded. Of course he would, as he had always protected her since she was a tiny orphaned child searching in vain for the parents who were no more.

The first blizzard of the season caught the villagers unawares while a hunting party was still out in the bush. Three out of the four hunters made it back to the village two hours after the storm hit, shivering and half-frozen, but alive. The fourth hunter—Grey Fox—had become separated from the others and was feared dead.

For three days, while the blizzard raged outside,

Moonflower, Summer Moon, and Dancing Caribou huddled speechlessly in their lodge, fearing the worst. At dawn on the fourth day, the blizzard ceased, and Summer Moon instantly entreated her son and the men of the village to search for her grandson. The men left immediately, and it had barely reached midday when they returned, bearing a frost-bitten, delirious young man whom they had found huddled under the bank of a frozen creek. Parts of his face and hands were blackened, and the skin sagged away from the rest, as if it were about to peel off. Moonflower wept when she saw her brother. She and her grandmother laid him carefully on his bed so they could tend to his wounds.

Summer Moon removed his ice-caked outer garments, but when she tried to unlace his boots, Grey Fox reared up and batted her hands away, screaming out and becoming so agitated that his grandmother was forced to leave the boots upon his feet. Moonflower took soft animal skins and dried the boots off as best she could, and then they gently treated his frostbitten face, hands, and torso with a special herbal remedy that Summer Moon always kept on hand during the winter.

All day and all night Grey Fox tossed and turned, his fever growing worse and worse. For a week his illness raged on, and the women and older men of the village took turns tending the ill warrior so that Moonflower and Summer Moon could sleep. On the fifth evening, the young warrior sat bolt upright, just as he had when Summer Moon tried to take off his boots, and screamed: "My feet of fire! My burning feet of fire!"

At his words, Summer Moon reeled back as if she had been struck. Moonflower, in the process of reaching to comfort her brother, stared at her grandmother in surprise. Between them, Grey Fox subsided against the pillows, his body shaking with cold, his fever climbing once again.

"Go fetch your uncle," Summer Moon told the girl sharply. "Right now!"

Amazed and frightened by the intensity of her grandmother's words, the maiden obeyed. Dancing Caribou hurried to obey the summons, and he huddled on the far side of the lodge with her grandmother, listening to her soft speech while Moonflower tenderly wiped her elder brother's sweating face with a cloth.

Suddenly, Grey Fox's dark eyes snapped open, and he gazed up at his sister menacingly, his eyes fixed in hunger upon her throat. For a moment, a red flame appeared in each pupil, and he bared his teeth at her as if he wanted to rip her throat right out of her neck. Moonflower gave a little shriek of fright, dropping the cloth and springing away from her brother.

Summer Moon and Dancing Caribou whirled in time to see Grey Fox sit up, flaming red eyes fixed upon the shrinking form of his little sister. His ravaged mouth was fixed into the savage grin of a hunting wolf, and he reached out both hands as if to grab his sister and drag her away. In two swift strides, Dancing Caribou crossed the lodge and knocked his nephew out with one sharp blow to the temple. Moonflower cried out a second time, half in protest and half in fear.

"Wendigo," hissed Summer Moon, coming to stand beside her grandson. "Wendigo."

For a moment, Moonflower did not understand. And then, she realized that her beloved brother must have encountered the Wendigo when he was trapped in the blizzard, and it had possessed him.

From that moment, a careful watch was set over the stricken warrior. The women were never allowed to be alone with him, and the warriors who mounted guard did so with weapons at the ready.

At midday, one week from the day he was found in the snowbank, Grey Fox came to his senses at last. Summer Moon and Moonflower were summoned at once, and more than half the village crowded into their lodge.

"Grandmother, sister," Grey Fox greeted them softly, his brown eyes human once more. He motioned for them to keep their distance. "I fear this will be the last time I will be myself, so I must speak quickly."

Drawing a deep breath, he told them his story. "As I wandered lost in the blizzard," he began, "I smelled a sweet, rotten smell on the swirling air, and then the Wendigo appeared before me and called my name. It clutched me to it with a clawed arm and ran with me so fast that my feet were burned. Then it leapt up into the air with me, and we raced through the storm clouds until my feet were engulfed by a white-hot fire.

"At the close of the storm, the creature dropped me from a great height, and I fell onto my head in the snowdrift under the creek. My feet still burned to the touch, and when I removed my boots, I found that there were only broken stumps where my feet used to be. It was shortly after this that the warriors found me.

"Night and day since that moment, I have dreamed of the Wendigo, and slowly the hunger for human flesh has grown

WENDIGO

within me until it burns my very soul. Yet the heart within me grows colder and colder, until I fear it will turn to ice. And I know that I have become a Wendigo myself."

Grey Fox drew in another deep breath when he finished his story. He looked first at his sister, then his grandmother, and then his uncle. "It is my dying wish that you kill this body immediately, in order to preserve the safety of our village and my family. Burn it until there is nothing left, and so banish the Wendigo from among you. Promise me that you will do this."

Moonflower made a small cry of protest, but Summer Moon and Dancing Caribou nodded their acquiescence. Summer Moon had foreseen this event at the moment she had heard his delirious cry.

"One thing more," Gray Fox said. "The Wendigo will not rest once it has lost my body as its host. It will take on its own deformed body and will prey upon the village throughout the coming months. You must summon Storm Hunter and his warriors to the village while there is still time, so that he may defeat the Wendigo."

A murmur went through the tent at his words. Storm Hunter was the mightiest warrior of their people. He lived in a village many leagues south of their tiny camp, but his fame had spread up and down the region. If anyone could defeat a Wendigo, it would be him.

"We will summon Storm Hunter," Dancing Caribou promised his nephew. Grey Fox nodded, his face sagging a bit as weariness overcame him. Sweat beaded his forehead once more.

"The Wendigo rises within me," he gasped, clutching

weakly at his heart. "Uncle, do what you must."

Dancing Caribou nodded again, too sorrowful to speak, as his nephew sagged back among the animal skins in a dead faint. The women were gently escorted out of the lodge, and the counsel of elders was summoned. An hour later, Grey Fox was executed by his uncle, as he had requested, and his body was burned in the very hottest fire that they could create at the center of the village, until not even one bone of him was left.

An hour later, the very swiftest messenger in the village departed for the south, to call upon Storm Hunter for aid before the winter storms closed in upon them, and the Wendigo with it.

The second blizzard hit a few days before the coming of the dark. It lasted for four days, and during that time, a hole was punched in the side of one of the lodges at the outskirts of the village, and two small children were dragged out into the storm. When the blizzard ceased, the warriors were sent to search for them. Their half-eaten corpses were recovered a mile outside of the village. The bodies were encircled by the bloody footprints of a two-legged creature with clawed feet. Wendigo.

A counsel was held in the chief's lodge, and it was decided to leave several homes empty at the outer edge of the village and move everyone into four of the largest and most easily defendable lodges at the center. Warriors would be posted at each lodge and would watch over the villagers in shifts during the next blizzard. And so it was.

The third blizzard lasted only two days, but they were long and tense days, filled with unspoken fears. And one man's name was on every villager's lips as the storm beat and howled around them. Storm Hunter. Storm Hunter. Had their messenger reached him? Would he come?

On the second night, a mighty roaring and thumping came from outside the lodges, accompanied by a sweet, rotten stench that turned the stomachs of all who smelt it. Again and again, something massive flung itself against the domiciles. The warriors shouted and thrust spears through the walls, and one brave soul leapt into the swirling, maddening darkness of the storm with a blazing torch, which was instantly blown from his hand and doused. The frightened villagers heard him give one strangled shout, and then the attack ceased as abruptly as it had started. The warrior did not return to the lodge, and they knew the Wendigo had claimed another victim. His body was never found.

In the calm between storms, in the few hours of daylight that remained during this shortest time of their year, a party of warriors emerged from the woods to the south of the village, accompanied by the village messenger. Among them was an exceptionally tall man with rugged features and sparkling amber eyes. He was not handsome, but he was so striking in appearance and charismatic in manner that no one noticed his lack of good looks beyond the first moment of meeting. He was Storm Hunter—so named because the year before he reached manhood, he had gone out in a raging blizzard and had tracked down a brace of sheltering caribou, killing three of them, and bringing the meat back to his village before storm's end to feed his starving people.

Moonflower hung back shyly as the warrior and his men were introduced to the villagers and told the story of the camp's fight against the Wendigo. But Storm Hunter seemed to sense her presence at the fringes of the crowd. When the tale of her poor possessed brother was related, his eyes met hers across the crowd. Such was the sympathy and distress that she read in his gaze that her heart was instantly bound to his, and she was comforted for the first time since her brother's death.

A place was offered to the great warrior in all four of the main lodges, but he chose to stay with Summer Moon, since she and her lovely granddaughter had been the first to feel the sting of the Wendigo. A feast was held that night to welcome the warrior, but it was interrupted by the onset of a fifth storm, and with it the coming of the Wendigo.

The beast attacked the village only a few hours after the blizzard began, howling and thumping against first one lodge and then the next. The brave warriors—both villagers and guests—thrust spears at its bulk and roared their defiance as the sweet, rotten stench of the creature filled the village.

Suddenly, a great claw tore a hole in the side of the lodge sheltering Moonflower, Summer Moon, and their relatives. A dark, foul, skeletal silhouette filled the gap as wind and snow gusted into the lodge. The creature's clawed hands gripped Moonflower around the leg and began dragging her out of the lodge, but Storm Hunter flung himself forward, a flaming torch in his hand. He thrust it into the face of the Wendigo, and the creature let go of the girl and leapt backward into the storm with inhuman speed. Two warriors ran forward to plug the gaping hole with blankets while Storm Hunter picked up the injured girl and carried her to the fire at the center of the lodge, to be tenderly nursed by her grandmother.

Though the warriors stayed alert during the rest of the five-day blizzard, the Wendigo did not come again.

The morning after the blizzard, Storm Hunter gathered his warriors together and made plans. They would not wait for the creature to come to the village. They were going to go right into its territory and set a trap. After spending most of the morning gathering supplies, the men set off for the deep woods where the Wendigo lay in wait for the next storm.

By midafternoon, Storm Hunter had found a clearing that contained the soft stench of the Wendigo, and at its far edge he built a hunting lean-to to persuade the creature that he was there to find game for the village. Facing him, and on both sides of the clearing, the warriors dug three pits for themselves in the deep drifts, and Storm Hunter covered them first with tarps and then with snow. Then he carefully smoothed the snow until it appeared as if no other hunter but himself had come to this solitary place.

At dusk, Storm Hunter lit a small fire, allowing it to blaze high enough to alert every creature in the vicinity to his presence before letting it die down. Then he retreated into the lean-to and sat with his back against the large trunk of a tree. He had crafted his shelter carefully so that the Wendigo could not attack from behind. He waited tensely, a smoldering torch ready by his side. One hour passed. Then two. Storm Hunter dozed a little, torch and spear held ready. It was his nose that finally told him the creature was close. The sweet, rotten smell of the Wendigo had grown nauseatingly strong within the clearing, and Storm Hunter took a deep breath and braced himself for the attack. Suddenly, the top of his shelter exploded inward as the creature leapt down upon it from the branches of the overhanging tree.

Storm Hunter leapt upward, thrusting the smoldering torch into the Wendigo's twisted, ravaged face and forcing it back with his spear. The creature leapt away from him to the side of the clearing with amazing speed, and instantly, the snow erupted behind it as the first group of warriors charged from their hiding place, spears and knives thrusting forward. The Wendigo fled to the opposite side of the clearing, only to be met by another group of screaming warriors. It headed for the gap between them, and came face-to-face with the third group.

The Wendigo gave an ear-splitting primeval scream that temporarily froze every warrior in his tracks. Then it leapt straight up in the air, straining to fly away from the unexpected danger. This was the moment for which Storm Hunter had been waiting. Bow in hand, he grabbed the arrow he had so carefully rubbed with flammable oil that afternoon, thrust it into the fire, and then knocked it onto his bow, all in one swift movement. Aiming for the Wendigo's icy heart, he shot straight and true. The arrow arched up and slammed through the creature's chest. The beast tumbled head over heels, screaming in agony, and spiraled to the ground like a leaf, landing headfirst in the snow as its whole body burst into flames.

For a long moment, the Wendigo burned, its figure flaring up as if it had been soaked with the same flammable oil as had Storm Hunter's arrow. The fire burned blood-red rather than yellow and smelled of rotting flesh. A thousand screaming spirits, their semitransparent bodies blue and pulsing, rushed upward to freedom out of the foul flames consuming the terrible creature and disappeared into the treetops above the warriors.

Then the Wendigo exploded, knocking all the warriors to the ground and sending a great cloud of smoke billowing up into the air. When the smoke cleared, Storm Hunter and his men climbed to their feet and looked around the darkened clearing. The Wendigo's body was completely obliterated, and a twenty-foot-long, three-foot-deep hole had been blasted into the ground. All the ice and snow in the clearing had boiled away, leaving only scorched, dry earth that swirled in strange dust patterns, the like of which the men had never seen.

Unwilling to stay in such an evil spot, the men retreated into the snowy woods and camped for the remainder of the night about a mile from the place where they had defeated the Wendigo. They returned in triumph to the village with the dawn, and a great feast was made in their honor.

Because of the danger of traveling long distances in the deep cold, Storm Hunter and his warriors spent the rest of the winter in the village, which remained blessedly free of incidents after the defeat of the Wendigo. In the spring, Storm Hunter and his men returned to their home in the south. With him, the warrior took his new bride, Moonflower, and Summer Moon and Dancing Caribou as well, since they could not bear to be parted from their only living relative.

While they never forgot the events of that terrible winter, neither the villagers nor Storm Hunter ever encountered another Wendigo.

Resources

Battle, Kemp P. *Great American Folklore*. New York: Doubleday & Company, Inc., 1986.

Bauchman, Rosemary, ed. *The Best of Helen Creighton*. Hantsport, Nova Scotia: Lancelot Press, 1988.

Botkin, B. A., ed. *A Treasury of American Folklore*. New York: Crown, 1944.

———. *A Treasury of Railroad Folklore*. New York: Crown, 1953.

Brewer, J. Mason. *American Negro Folklore*. Chicago, IL: Quadrangle Books, 1972.

Brunvand, Jan Harold. *The Choking Doberman and Other Urban Legends*. New York: W. W. Norton, 1984.

———. *The Vanishing Hitchhiker*. New York: W. W. Norton, 1981.

Christensen, Jo-Anne. *Ghost Stories of British Columbia*. Toronto, Ontario: Hounslow Press, 1996.

———. *Ghost Stories of Saskatchewan*. Toronto, Ontario: Hounslow Press, 1995.

————. *More Ghost Stories of Saskatchewan*. Edmonton, Alberta: Lone Pine, 2000.

Coffin, Tristram. P., and Hennig Cohen, eds. *Folklore in America*. New York: Doubleday & AMP, 1966.

————. *Folklore from the Working Folk of America*. New York: Doubleday, 1973.

Cohen, Daniel. *Ghostly Tales of Love & Revenge*. New York: Putnam Publishing Group, 1992.

Cohen, Daniel, and Susan Cohen. *Hauntings & Horrors*. New York: Dutton Children's Books, 2002.

Colombo, John Robert. *Ghost Stories of Canada*. Toronto, Ontario: Hounslow Press, 2000.

————. *Mysteries of Ontario*. Toronto, Ontario: Hounslow Press, 1999.

Dorson, R. M. *America in Legend*. New York: Pantheon Books, 1973.

Earle, George H. *A Collection of Foolishness & Folklore*. St. John's, Newfoundland: Harry Cuff Publications Ltd., 1988.

Editors of LIFE. *The LIFE Treasury of American Folklore*. New York: Time Inc., 1961.

Erdoes, Richard, and Alfonso Ortiz. *American Indian Myths and Legends*. New York: Pantheon Books, 1984.

Ferrell, Ed. *Strange Stories of Alaska and the Yukon*. Fairbanks, Alaska: Epicenter Press, 1996.

Flanagan, J. T., and A. P. Hudson. *The American Folk Reader*. New York: A. S. Barnes & Co., 1958.

Fraser, Mary L. *Folklore of Nova Scotia*. Antigonish, Nova Scotia: Formac Limited, 1928.

Freygood, Steven. *Headless George and Other Tales Told in Canada*. Toronto, Ontario: Key Porter Books, 1983.

Fowke, Edith. *Folklore of Canada*. Toronto, Ontario: McClelland and Stewart Limited, 1976.

———. *Legends Told in Canada*. Toronto, Ontario: Royal Ontario Museum, 1994.

Greenough, William Parker. *Canadian Folk-Life and Folk-Lore*. Amsterdam, The Netherlands: Fredonia Books, 2002.

Hervy, Sheila. *Canada Ghost to Ghost*. Toronto, Ontario: Stoddart Publishing Co. Limited, 1996.

———. *Some Canadian Ghosts*. Markham, Ontario: Simon & Schuster of Canada, 1973.

Jarvis, Dale. *Haunted Shores*. St. John's, Newfoundland: Flanker Press, Ltd., 2004.

Johnson, E. Pauline. *Legends of Vancouver*. Alsbury, Bucks, England: McClelland and Steward Limited, 1920.

Klymasz, Robert B. *Folk Narrative Among Ukrainian–Canadians in Western Canada*. Ottawa, Ontario: Canadian Centre for Folk Culture Studies, 1973.

Lambert, R. S. *Exploring the Supernatural.* Toronto, Ontario: McClelland and Stewart Limited, 1955.

Leach, M. *The Rainbow Book of American Folk Tales and Legends.* New York: The World Publishing Co., 1958.

Leeming, David, and Jake Page. *Myths, Legends, & Folktales of America.* New York: Oxford University Press, 1999.

Manguel, Alberto, ed. *The Oxford Book of Canadian Ghost Stories.* Toronto, Ontario: Oxford University Press, 1990.

Nungak, Zebedee, and Eugene Arima. *Inuit Stories.* Hull, Quebec: Canadian Museum of Civilization, 1988.

Peck, Catherine, ed. *A Treasury of North American Folk Tales.* New York: W. W. Norton, 1998.

Polley, J., ed. *American Folklore and Legend.* New York: Reader's Digest Association, 1978.

Schwartz, Alvin. *Scary Stories to Tell in the Dark.* New York: Harper Collins, 1981.

Service, Robert W. Best *Tales of the Yukon.* Philadelphia, PA: Running Press, 1983.

Sherwood, Roland H. *Maritime Mysteries.* Hantsport, Nova Scotia: Lancelot Press Limited, 1995.

Skinner, Charles M. *American Myths and Legends*, Vol. 1. Philadelphia: J. B. Lippincott, 1903.

———. *Myths and Legends Beyond Our Borders.* Philadelphia: J. B. Lippincott, 1899.

Smith, Barbara. *Canadian Ghost Stories.* Edmonton, Alberta: Lone Pine, 2001.

———. *Ghost Stories of Alberta.* Toronto, Ontario: Hounslow Press, 1993.

———. *Ghost Stories of Manitoba.* Edmonton, Alberta: Lone Pine, 1998.

———. *More Ghost Stories of Alberta.* Edmonton, Alberta: Lone Pine, 1996.

Spence, Lewis. *North American Indians: Myths and Legends Series.* London: Bracken Books, 1985.

Stone, Ted, ed. *13 Canadian Ghost Stories.* Saskatoon, Saskatchewan: Western Producer Prairie Books, 1988.

Stonehouse, Frederick. *Haunted Lakes.* Duluth, MN: Lake Superior Port Cities, Inc., 1997.

———. *Haunted Lakes II.* Duluth, MN: Lake Superior Port Cities, Inc., 2000.

Watson, Julie V. *Ghost Stories & Legends of Prince Edward Island.* Toronto, Ontario: Hounslow Press, 1988.

Zeitlin, Steven J., Amy J. Kotkin, and Holly Cutting Baker. *A Celebration of American Family Folklore.* New York: Pantheon Books, 1982.

About the Author

S. E. Schlosser has been telling stories since she was a child, when games of "let's pretend" quickly built themselves into full-length tales acted out with friends. A graduate of Houghton College, the Institute of Children's Literature, and Rutgers University, she created and maintains the award-winning Web site Americanfolklore.net, where she shares a wealth of stories from all fifty states, some dating back to the origins of America. Sandy spends much of her time answering questions from visitors to the site. Many of her favorite e-mails come from other folklorists who delight in practicing the old tradition of who can tell the tallest tale.